WebPlus X7
Resource Guide

Contacting Serif

Help with your Product

ComMunityPlus

community.serif.com
Get answers and ask questions in the Serif community!

Serif Support

www.serif.com/support
For Serif Account and Customer Service information.

Additional Serif information

Serif website

www.serif.com

Main office

Address	The Software Centre, PO Box 2000 Nottingham, NG11 7GW, UK
Phone	(0115) 914 2000
Phone (Registration)	(0800) 376 1989 +44 800 376 1989 800-794-6876 (US, Canada)
Phone (Sales)	(0800) 376 7070 +44 800 376 7070 800-489-6703 (US, Canada)
Customer Service	0845 345 6770 800-489-6720 (US, Canada)
Fax	(0115) 914 2020

Credits

This Resource Guide, and the software described in it, is furnished under an end user License Agreement, which is included with the product. The agreement specifies the permitted and prohibited uses.

Trademarks

Serif is a registered trademark of Serif (Europe) Ltd.

WebPlus is a registered trademark of Serif (Europe) Ltd.

All Serif product names are trademarks of Serif (Europe) Ltd.

Microsoft, Windows, and the Windows logo are registered trademarks of Microsoft Corporation. All other trademarks acknowledged.

Windows Vista and the Windows Vista Start button are trademarks or registered trademarks of Microsoft Corporation in the United States and/or other countries.

Google+ social service, Google Analytics web analytics service, and Google AdSense advertising service are trademarks of Google Inc.

Copyrights

Introduction

Welcome to the WebPlus X7 Resource Guide.

This Resource Guide covers the best techniques for using the fundamental tools in WebPlus, from beginner- to advanced-level, and provides creative inspiration for producing a website.

1: Tutorials

This chapter will introduce you to the basics of getting your site up and running. We'll show you how to get started with a template, how to insert text and pictures, add site navigation, use panels, sliders and forms, and make your site accessible to mobile devices and search engines. We'll also provide tips on publishing your site.

2: Creative Showcase

Be inspired by the work in this chapter! We showcase a few Pro Templates and Theme Layouts alongside examples created using assets and object styles. Instructions on accessing these templates and theme layouts are also included.

Working with tutorials

Throughout the Resource Guide, you'll be prompted to access resource files from within WebPlus. These files have been provided to get you started or to help focus on a key learning point. Details for accessing these files are provided within the tutorial.

You will need to enable Javascript in your chosen browser to preview some of the features discussed in the Resource Guide.

Useful icons

Here is a quick guide to the icons you'll find useful along the way.

 Don't forget to save your work! We'll remind you along the way with these helpful save points.

 These give you an estimate of how long a tutorial will take to complete.

 For guidance, tutorials are graded between 1 (beginner) - 5 (advanced).

 This is a note. Notes provide useful information about the program or a particular technique.

 This is a tip. Our tips provide information that will help you with your projects.

 This is a warning! We don't want to make you panic but when you see this icon, you need to pay attention to the steps as they will be particularly important.

Exploring WebPlus X7

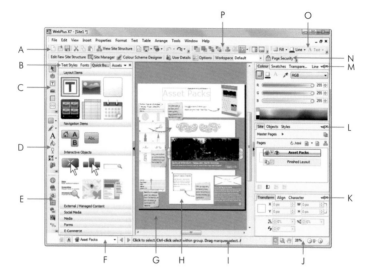

(**A**) Standard toolbar, (**B**) Text Styles, Fonts, Quick Build, and Assets tabs, (**C**) Basic toolbar, (**D**) Drawing toolbar, (**E**) Properties toolbar, (**F**) Page Locator, (**G**) Pasteboard area, (**H**) Page area, (**I**) Hintline toolbar, (**J**) View options, (**K**) Transform, Align, and Character tabs, (**L**) Site, Objects, and Styles tabs, (**M**) Colour, Swatches, Transparency, and Line tabs, (**N**) Context toolbar, (**O**) Colour toolbar, (**P**) Arrange toolbar.

Table of Contents

Tutorials

1

New site from template

 15-20 min

Creating a website in WebPlus can be as simple as choosing and customizing a design template, a theme layout (as in this example), or you can start from scratch. The building blocks that go on to make up your website are saved as a project file which will eventually be published to the internet for all to see.

By the end of this tutorial you will be able to:

* Open a Theme Layout template.

* Preview your template site.

* Add template pages using the Site and Assets tabs.

* Add a new blank page.

* Add page content using the Assets tab.

Let's begin...

1. From the **File** menu, click **Startup Assistant**.

2. On the left, click **Templates**.

3. On the **Templates** list, select **Theme Layouts**, and from the thumbnail gallery, select the **Aperture** template.

   The gallery updates to display the template's colour scheme and pages.

4. From the right thumbnail gallery:

- From the **Colour Scheme** drop-down list, select a scheme for your site—we've kept to the default scheme.

- Click **OK**.

The 'Home' page is displayed in the workspace with the **Assets** tab populated with all the theme's assets.

To save your work:

1. Before proceeding, click **File**, then **Save As**.

2. Save your project file with a file name of your choice.

> Saving the WebPlus (.wpp) project file allows you to return to your work at a later date to make changes. It is not the same as publishing it to the internet as a full website. See the *Publishing your site* tutorial on p. 171 for more details about publishing your site once it is complete.

Previewing your website

With a wide selection of web browsers available, it's important to test your site to ensure that it will be viewed in the way that you intended. Before you upload your site to the masses, we'll show you how to test your site in different browsers.

To preview your site in WebPlus:

1.  On the **Standard** toolbar, click the arrow to expand the **Preview site** drop-down list.

2. Click the **Preview in Window (Internet Explorer)** option.

    Once exported, WebPlus displays the site preview in a built-in Microsoft Internet Explorer window.

3. To switch between your regular design view and the **Preview**, simply click on the tabs at the top of the workspace area.

4. Even if your site navigation is incomplete, you can jump to different pages using the Page Locator at the bottom left of the workspace.

Checking your site with different screen resolutions is easy in the **Preview** window. Simply pick another preview size in the drop-down list on the context toolbar.

5. When you have finished previewing your site, click **Close Preview**.

If you make any changes to your design, your site will be 'republished' when you next switch to **Preview**. You can also preview your site in an actual browser window. This is useful for testing compatibility with other browsers such as Firefox, Chrome, Safari or Opera. WebPlus automatically detects if alternate browsers are installed.

To preview your site in a browser:

1.   ![icon] On the **Standard** toolbar, click the arrow to expand the **Preview site** drop-down list.

2.   Select **Preview in {your web browser of choice}**.

WebPlus generates the necessary temporary files and opens a new browser window displaying the site's Home page.

The navigation bar (highlighted) interconnects the site's pages and is an indispensable element of site design. Users will expect it to be there, they'll know what to do with it, and it will help them grasp your site's structure at a glance.

3.   Close the browser when you've finished.

> Though statistics vary, the most popular browsers are Google Chrome, Firefox and Internet Explorer. Other browsers such as Opera (especially for mobile devices) and Safari are also supported by WebPlus. Each browser works differently so it's important to see how your site appears in each of them. For more information search *Previewing your site* in WebPlus Help.

Next we'll look at adding pages.

Adding template pages

Your website will grow and change with your needs and you can add pages as you go. Blank pages can be added, but they need populating with content, which can be time consuming. More conveniently, you can add new template pages to your site. They come populated with professionally designed page content, saving you lots of time!

To add a new asset page:

1. On the **Assets** tab, click the **Pages** category header to display the template's Page assets.

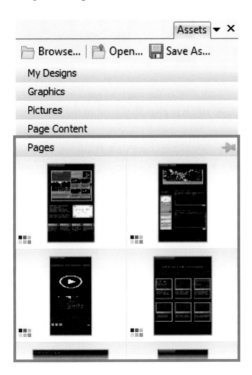

2.   Drag a page onto the workspace, and drop it (by releasing the mouse button) to the right of the current page when a large arrow appears.

The page is added after the current page in the Site tab and listed as 'Page 10'. It is also displayed in the workspace.

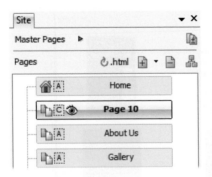

3.   On the **Site** tab, right-click **Page 10** and select **Page Properties**.

4. In the **Page Properties** dialog, in the **Navigation** category, type 'Bookings' into the **Page name** box, then click **OK**.

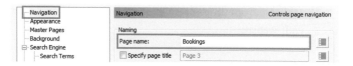

Now we've added a new page, let's see how it looks by previewing the site in a web browser. (For a reminder, see *To preview your site in a browser* on p. 8.)

As you can see, the navigation bar has automatically updated to accommodate your new pages.

Once you've experimented with the navigation bar, close the browser window and return to WebPlus.

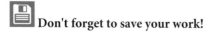 **Don't forget to save your work!**

Adding a new blank page

You can quickly construct site pages by adding page content assets
available from the **Assets** tab. First, you'll need to add a new page to
your website.

To add a new blank page:

1. On the **Site** tab, click the arrow on the ⊞ ▾ **Add new page or
    link** drop-down list and select **New Blank Page**.

2. In the **Page Properties** dialog, in the **Navigation** category:

    • In the **Naming** section, type in a page name, title, and file
      name—we chose to create an 'Events' page.

    • In the **Placement** section, select **After** and then, from the
      drop-down list, select **Bookings**.

    • Click **OK**.

Your new blank page opens in the workspace and is positioned after
the 'Bookings' page in the navigation bar and **Site** tab.

The new page automatically adopts all the page elements placed on the **Master A** page. This is indicated in the **Site** tab.

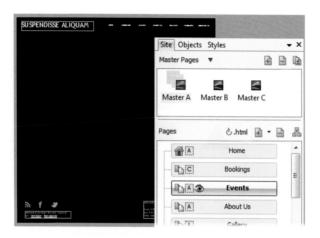

Search *Understanding pages and master pages* in WebPlus Help for more details on using Master pages.

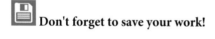 **Don't forget to save your work!**

Adding page content

Now, we'll add a shape to this new page so it fits with the theme of the other pages on the site. This asset can be found in the Graphics category of the **Assets** tab.

To add a graphic asset to a page:

1. On the **Assets** tab, click the **Graphics** category header to display the template's graphic assets.

2. Drag the **Banner** tagged asset from the **Assets** tab onto the page.

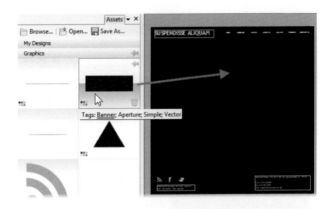

Asset tags are displayed by hovering the mouse over the asset thumbnail.

3. With the object still selected, drag on the top- and bottom-centre control handles to resize the shape to fill most of the page.

4.   On the **Align** tab, click Centre Horizontally to display the shape neatly on the page.

Now let's populate the page with page content!

To add page content assets to a page:

1.   On the **Assets** tab, click the **Page Content** category header to display the template's Page Content assets.

2.   Drag any page content asset directly onto the page.

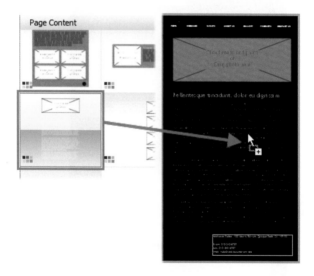

The page content is added to the page and remains selected.

Chances are you won't position the asset perfectly first time, so you may wish to reposition (and possibly resize) it once it is on the page.

To reposition and resize assets:

1. With the Page Content asset still selected, click and drag the ⊕ button to reposition the content on the page.

   As you drag the content, dynamic guides will appear to allow you to line up content with the page (blue lines) or other content (red lines).

To select page content, simply click and drag from the grey pasteboard and draw a marquee around the content you want to select.

2. Click the corner or side handles and drag them to resize page content as required.

3. Drag additional page content items from the **Assets** tab onto the page, and reposition and resize as necessary.

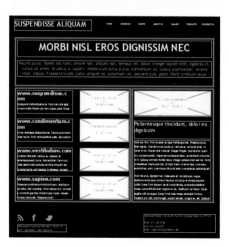

Your website is now ready to be populated with pictures, text, and hyperlinks!

 Don't forget to save your work!

 Pictures, text, and hyperlinks are so important when building a website, we have dedicated tutorials for each of them, and therefore they are not discussed here. See the *Frame text*, *Framed pictures*, and *Creating hyperlinks and anchors* tutorials on p. 29, p. 39, and p. 53, respectively, for more details.

With your website populated with custom pictures, text, and hyperlinks, all you need to do now is publish it to the internet! See the *Publishing your site* tutorial on p. 171 for more details.

Modifying site structure

 15-20 min

Using WebPlus, it's easy to design clearly structured websites that are quick and simple to navigate. In this tutorial, we'll use a WebPlus template to introduce you to the basic elements of site structure as well as showing you how the Site Structure view can help you organize your site.

By the end of this tutorial you will be able to:

• Navigate between pages.

• Change navigation preferences.

• Rearrange pages.

• Create child pages.

Let's begin...

• Open the **Aperture** template as described on p. 4.

 If you have already completed the previous tutorial, you can use your saved project for this tutorial.

Navigating your site's structure

When you build your website, it's important for you to have an understanding of site structure and its hierarchy. This is a fundamental part of website design and helps you to create a site that visitors will be able to navigate easily.

To begin with, we'll have a look at the Site tab.

To navigate between pages:

1. At the right of the workspace, click the **Site** tab.

    This tab displays the **Site Structure tree** for this particular site. You'll recognize the entries as the main pages of the site.

2. On the **Site** tab, double-click a page entry to open it in the workspace.

As you change pages, notice that the ⚙ icon moves to indicate which page is currently in view and ready for editing.

Next we'll enter into Site Structure view to examine and amend the structure of the template's site.

Site Structure view

The Site Structure view is a great visual map of your site's structure—it's perfect for larger sites. Let's look at this now.

To open Site Structure view:

- On the **Site** tab, click ⬚ **Site Structure**.

  The **Site Structure** view opens as a new tab allowing you to quickly switch between this view and the main workspace.

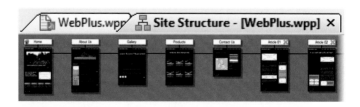

Once in Site Structure view, you can easily begin to manage the structure of your site.

Changing site navigation

If all of your pages were included in the site navigation, on a large website the navigation would be almost unusable. In WebPlus it's easy to specify whether or not a page is included.

In WebPlus, pages that are not included in the navigation have an 'x' next to their names.

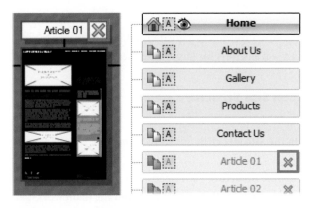

Site Structure view (left) and Site tab (right)

If you preview the site in a browser, you can see this from the navigation bar. See *To preview your site in a browser* on p. 8 for details.

By default, all new pages added to your site are included in navigation bars. You can, however, exclude any pages from your navigation bar at any time.

To change navigation options:

1. In **Site Structure** view, click to select the **About Us** page.

2. On the context toolbar, deselect  **Include in Navigation**.

The About Us page now displays an 'x' beside its name and if you preview your site again, you will notice About Us is no longer listed.

Switching off the **Include in Navigation** setting for a page forces navigation bars to ignore that page, and its button disappears.

To include an excluded page in navigation, simply repeat the steps listed above.

You can select multiple pages in Site Structure view (press the **Ctrl** key while clicking pages) and then exclude them all from the navigation bar in one go.

You can also move pages around within the site structure tree so they display in a different order in the navigation bar. We'll look at this next.

 Save now! Click **File > Save As**.

Page order

You can organize pages by dragging the selected page thumbnail to a new location. As you drag over a target page, square handles appear to help you position the page correctly, either next to the target page or as a child page of it.

To change page order:

1. In **Site Structure** view, click to select the **Products** page.

2. Drag the **Products** page over the **Gallery** page and release the mouse button when the left square handle changes colour.

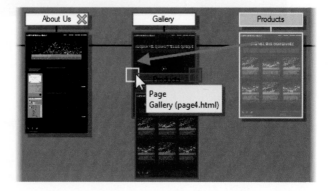

As this page is included in the navigation, the navigation bar updates automatically to mirror the new top-level page order. If you preview your site again, you will notice Products is now listed to the left of Gallery.

If a page has child pages, these also move as they are dependent on the parent page. We'll discuss child pages next.

 Don't forget to save your work!

Child pages

A parent-and-child 'tree' structure provides a natural framework for organizing site content into sections and levels. This site currently has one main page at the top level for each of our main sections. Over time we would expect to add subsidiary (child) pages to each section. Let's do this now.

To add a new child page:

1. In **Site Structure** view, click to select the **Products** page.

2. On the context toolbar, click **Insert Page**.

3.   In the **Page Properties** dialog, on the **Navigation** option:

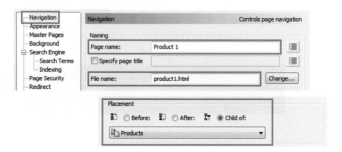

- In the **Page name** text box, type 'Product 1'.

- Change the **File name** to 'product1.html'.

- In the **Placement** section, select the **Child of** option.

- Click **OK**.

A new page opens in the workspace and a new entry is displayed in Site Structure view. The new page is connected underneath the Products page, i.e., it's a child of the Products page as we specified in the dialog.

4.   Preview the site in a browser.

If you hover over the Products item in the navigation bar, you'll now see a Product 1 item appear in the flyout (drop-down menu).

Having inserted a new page in the Products section of the site, we now have the makings of a hierarchy. The lines connecting the page entries make more sense—the site structure has now taken on a tree diagram (or map) appearance.

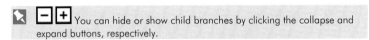 You can hide or show child branches by clicking the collapse and expand buttons, respectively.

You can also move an existing page to become a child page at any time.

To make an existing page a child page:

1. In **Site Structure** view, click to select the **Gallery** page.

2. Drag the **Gallery** page over the **Products** page and release the mouse button when the bottom square handle changes colour.

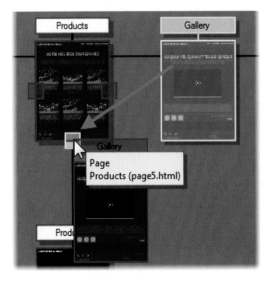

The site structure tree updates to accommodate the additional child page.

As this page is included in the navigation, the navigation bar updates automatically to mirror the new site structure. If you preview your site again, you will notice Gallery has disappeared from the top of the navigation bar and is now listed under Products.

That's it! We've reached the end of this tutorial on modifying site structure. You should now understand a little about site structure and how navigation bars adapt instantly to changes in the structure. See the *Navigation bars* tutorial on p. 67 for more details.

You can also use the Site tab to adjust your site structure. Search *Site tab* and *Understanding site structure* in WebPlus Help for more information.

Frame text

 15 min

There are two types of text in WebPlus—Artistic and frame. Each type has different properties, allowing you to create great looking websites. To make your site as accessible as possible, you should use **text frames** for all main body text content. In this tutorial we'll look at how you can use text frames to add text content to your website.

By the end of this tutorial you will be able to:

- Edit existing text frames.

- Create text frames.

- Insert placeholder text.

- Format text frames.

- Apply text styles.

Let's begin...

* Open the **Aperture** template as described on p. 4.

 If you have already completed the previous tutorial, you can use your saved project for this tutorial.

All WebPlus theme layouts (and Pro Templates) are populated with placeholder text frames that you can use as starting points for your own site. We'll look at editing these first and then move onto adding your own text frames.

Editing existing frame text

All of the text on the Home page of the Aperture template is contained within text frames. This allows us to quickly personalize the template while keeping the textual structure of the page in place.

To select, edit and format text:

1. Click anywhere within the text frame which starts 'MORBI NISL' and then press **Ctrl+A**.

All the text within the text frame is selected.

2.   Type 'Welcome'.

The text overwrites the placeholder text. It will appear as upper-case text as specified by the applied text style.

On the context toolbar, in the styles drop-down list, select **Heading 1**.

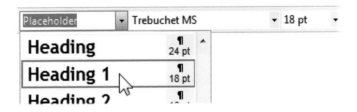

The heading is updated.

As we've reduced the word count, the frame now looks excessively large. We can resize this to give us more room for other page objects.

 Save now! Click **File > Save As**.

To resize a frame by dragging:

1. Move the mouse pointer over the frame's bottom-centre handle. The pointer will change to a double-headed arrow.

2. Click and drag to resize the frame so that its height spans that of the 'Welcome' text.

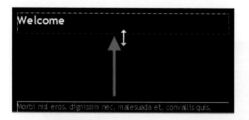

If you drag the text frame too far the 'Welcome' text will shrink to allow it to still be read.

3. Click anywhere within the text frame which starts 'Morbi nisl eros'.

4. Move the mouse pointer over the frame's top-centre handle. The pointer will change to a double-headed arrow.

5. Click and drag to resize the frame so that it stretches up the page, opening up extra space for additional text.

You can now replace the placeholder text with your personalized copy using the directions above.

 If you have already prepared your website's text in a text editor, you can copy it directly into a text frame using a variety of methods (including Copy and Paste). Search *Putting text into a frame* in WebPlus Help for more details.

Next we'll show you how to add a new text frame to your site.

Creating text frames

WebPlus makes it easy to quickly add text frames to a page. However, the Home page is currently full and so we'll need to first make some space for the text frame. We'll do this by removing the placeholder picture frame.

To delete a page object:

• Click to select the placeholder picture frame and then press the **Delete** key.

Now we'll place our text frame in the vacated space.

To place a text frame:

1. On the **Quick Build** tab, in the **Layout Items** category, click the **Text Frame** layout item.

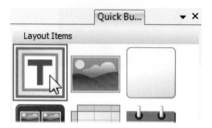

2. With the  cursor, drag on the page to insert the frame at a size which fills the vacated space.

To save time when designing a site, you can fill any text frame with placeholder text. This can help you (or your client) to visualise the overall design before the actual content is added. Let's now fill our frame with some text.

To create placeholder text:

1. Click inside the text frame to create an insertion point.

2. From the **Text** menu, click **Insert>Fill with Placeholder Text**.

Why not format the text frame so that it creates an attractive container? We'll look at how you can do this next.

Formatting text frames

Over the next few steps we'll apply a fill and padding to the newly added text frame.

To change the fill colour of a text frame:

1. Click the text frame border to select the text frame (the border will turn to a solid outline).

2. On the Swatches tab, click the 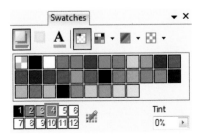 **Fill** button and then select **Scheme Colour 4**.

As you can see, the text goes right up to the edges of the frame. Now that we've added colour this doesn't look as good. We can improve things dramatically by adding some external padding to the frame.

To add external padding:

1. Ensure that the text frame is selected and then, from the **Properties** menu, select **CSS Properties**.

2. In the dialog:

- On the **Padding** tab, set the **Left** and **Top** padding to **10** pix.

  By default the **Right** and **Bottom** padding are linked to the **Left** and **Top** padding, respectively, and will update to match.

- Click **OK**.

The frame is updated.

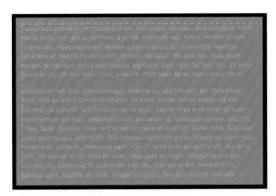

The text colour and the text frame colour we chose clash, making it difficult to read the text. We'll change the text format using a text style.

To format text using text styles:

1. Click anywhere within the text frame and then press **Ctrl+A**.

2. On the **Text Styles** tab, select **Body 2**.

The style is applied to the text.

Maecenas condimentum tincidunt lorem. Vestibulum velit elus. Sed vulputate. Morbi massa nunc, convallis a, commodo gravida, tincidunt sed, turpis. Aenean ornare viverra est. Maecenas lorem. Aenean euismod iaculis dui. Cum sodis natoque penatibus et magnis dis parturient montes, nascetur ridiculus mus. Nulla quam. Aenean fermentum, turpis sed volutpat dignissim, diam risus facilisis nibh, sit amet iaculis est turpis non tellus. Nunc a mauris. Proin eget ligula. Nam cursus libero.

Vestibulum velit orci, bibendum eget, molestie eu, sagittis non, leo. Nullam sed enim. Duis ac lorem. Lorem ipsum dolor sit amet, consectetuer adipiscing elit. Suspendisse potenti. Sed tincidunt varius arcu. Mauris vitae arcu sit amet quam condimentum pulvinar. Aenean arcu elit, accumsan id, consequat ornare, lobortis vitae, ligula. Quisque vitae velit ac sapien placerat suscipit. Donec mollis justo sed justo pellentesque sollicitudin. Duis bibendum adipiscing nibh. Maecenas diam risus, molestie ut, porta et, malesuada eget, nisl. In fermentum leo sed turpis. Sed lacus velit, consequat in, ultricies sit amet, malesuada et, diam. Integer mauris sem, convallis ut, consequat in, sollicitudin sed, leo. Cras purus elit, hendrerit ut, egestas eget, sagittis at, nulla. Integer justo dui, faucibus dictum, convallis

That's it! We've reached the end of this tutorial on frame text. We've covered many useful tips for creating, editing, and managing text with WebPlus. We hope that you're now feeling ready to get started with creating content for your own site!

Throughout the tutorial we encouraged you to use text styles. If you use styles to format text, you have the advantage that if you want to change the style, all instances of that formatting also update. Text styles also keep your website looking consistent. If you do decide to overwrite the format of the text style with local formatting, we recommend selecting a font from the **Fonts** tab's Websafe list for best possible results.

 Don't forget to save your work!

Framed pictures

 30 min

Using pictures is a great way to create an eye-catching website. However, used incorrectly, they can slow the loading of your site and frustrate visitors. WebPlus has a few tricks for placing pictures while optimizing page download. We'll introduce you to these tricks for importing, placing, and managing pictures on your website.

By the end of this tutorial you will be able to:

- Use picture frames.

- Use pictures from the Assets tab.

- Add picture frames.

- Adjust pictures in frames.

- Create self-linking picture hyperlinks.

- Add ALT and TITLE text to pictures.

Let's begin...

- Open the **Aperture** template as described on p. 4.

 If you have already completed the previous tutorial, you can use your saved project for this tutorial.

All WebPlus theme layouts are populated with placeholder picture frames waiting to accommodate your pictures.

Using picture frames

Placing picture frames on your site pages has several benefits:

- You can use empty frames as 'placeholder' areas when you know you want to add pictures, but have yet to put them in.

- Frames make it easy to place pictures at a specific size or shape, without changing the aspect ratio—useful for 'contact' pictures or thumbnails.

- You can easily swap the pictures displayed inside frames without altering the page layout.

You can add pictures individually by clicking directly on a picture frame, or you can add multiple pictures to the **Assets** tab and then drag them onto the frames as you need them. We'll demonstrate both methods. We'll be using the sample pictures installed with WebPlus. However, you can use your own pictures if you prefer.

To add a picture to a frame:

1. On the **Site** tab, double-click the **Article 01** page to open it in the workspace.

2. Select the top-left picture frame and then click **Replace Picture from Disk**.

3. In the **Import Picture** dialog, browse to your **Images** folder.

> In a standard installation, the image files can be accessed from the following location:
>
> C:\Program Files\Serif\WebPlus\X7\Images or
> C:\Program Files (x86)\Serif\WebPlus\X7\Images
>
> However, the path may differ if you changed the installation location.

4. Select **060510n0732.JPG** and click **Open**.

5. The picture is added to the frame and scaled to maximum-fit by default.

You can also add (or replace) a picture within a frame directly using a Picture asset.

> We've provided a convenient **Tutorial** asset pack which contains all the pictures you will need to help you progress through this tutorial.

To add a Picture asset to a frame:

1. Select the lower-left picture frame and then click 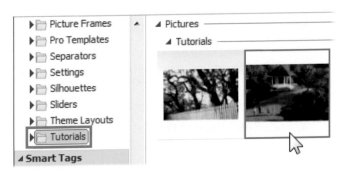 **Replace Picture from Assets**.

2. In the **Asset Browser**, from the **Pack Files** section, select **Installed Packs>Tutorials**.

3. Select the picture of the pagoda and click **OK**.

4. The picture is added to the frame and scaled to maximum-fit by default.

Now let's explore Picture assets and the Assets tab in more detail.

Using the Assets tab

WebPlus provides a selection of royalty-free pictures for you to use in your website. These can be quickly imported and conveniently stored in the Assets tab for easy access and quick addition to your site.

To add Picture assets to the Assets tab:

1. On the **Assets** tab, click 📁 **Browse** to open the **Asset Browser**.

2. In the **Categories** section, click to select the **Pictures** category. The pictures from all installed packs are displayed in the main pane.

3. In the main pane the assets are categorized by the Pack file that they belong to. In the **Tutorials** pack, click on the thumbnail of the trees.

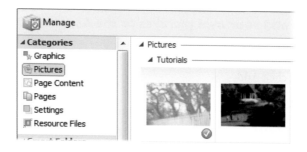

The green ✅ shows that the asset has been added to the tab.

4. Click **Close** to exit.

Our recently imported asset displays in the Pictures category on the
Assets tab.

You might prefer to add your own pictures to the Assets tab before
adding them to your site.

To add your own pictures to the Asset tab:

1. On the **Assets** tab, click the **Pictures** category header and then
    click **Add**.

2. In the **Import Picture** dialog, browse to the folder which
    contains your pictures and then select the pictures you want to
    import. (Use **Ctrl**- or **Shift**-click to select multiple pictures.)

3. Click **Open**.

Your pictures are imported directly into the Assets tab for use in
your current website. Now that we have imported a Picture asset, we
can add it to a picture frame.

To add a picture to a frame using the Assets tab:

1. On the **Assets** tab, the **Pictures** category should be displayed (if not, click the header).

2. Drag the picture onto the top-right picture frame.

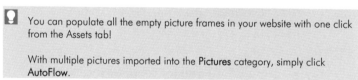
You can populate all the empty picture frames in your website with one click from the Assets tab!

With multiple pictures imported into the Pictures category, simply click AutoFlow.

Now we've shown you how to populate blank picture frames, let's look at adding a new blank picture frame.

 Save now! Click **File > Save As**.

Adding picture frames

If you're designing a page (or site) from scratch or modifying an existing page, you may wish to add picture frames to your page for the reasons highlighted above. You can also align picture frames with other objects on the page using dynamic guides.

> Dynamic guides allow you to align new objects to the last three selected page objects.

To use dynamic guides:

1. On the **Site** tab, double-click the **Article 02** page to open it in the workspace.

2. On the **Arrange** toolbar:

    - Ensure ⬆ **Snapping** is enabled (highlighted).

    - From the ⬆ ▾ **Snapping** flyout, ensure **Dynamic Guides** is enabled (highlighted).

3. Underneath the page's top-left empty space, click to select the text frame and then click to select the large blank picture frame to the right.

Now, we'll create a new picture frame...

To add a picture frame to the page:

1. On the **Quick Build** tab, in the **Layout Items** category,
    Ctrl-click the **Picture** layout item.

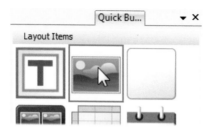

2. Position the ⊞ 🖼 cursor around the empty space. You should
    see the dynamic guides appear to help you position your picture
    frame.

3. Drag across and down to fill the empty space and add a blank
    picture frame.

You can now populate the picture frame by clicking **Replace
Picture from Disk** or **Replace Picture from Assets**, or dragging
pictures from the **Assets** tab (as previously discussed).

When a picture in a frame is selected, the Picture Frame toolbar displays in the lower-right corner. You can use these tools to adjust your picture inside the frame. We'll look at this next.

 Don't forget to save your work!

Adjusting framed pictures

The picture of the pagoda we added earlier is not ideally positioned within the frame. We can adjust this using the Picture Frame toolbar.

To reposition the picture inside the frame:

1. On the **Site** tab, double-click the **Article 01** page to open it in the workspace.

2. Click to select the pagoda picture and display the Picture frame toolbar.

3. Click **Position Image**, and then click and drag on the picture downwards with the pan cursor.

 Feel free to experiment with the other adjustments on the Picture Frame toolbar. Search *Adding picture frames* in WebPlus Help for details.

Now we've looked at placing pictures, let's look at a few ways we can optimize these pictures to improve a visitor's browsing experience.

Linking from a thumbnail to a larger picture

You can link to high-resolution pictures from thumbnails and display them in a professionally designed lightbox.

To display a picture in a lightbox:

1. Select the small picture of the trees on the **Article 01** page and then on the **Properties** toolbar, click **Hyperlink**.

2. In the dialog, on the **Hyperlink Type** tab (**Hyperlink** tab), select **Picture**.

3. On the **Target Window** tab, select **Lightbox** from the **Type** drop-down list.

4. Click **OK**.

Let's preview the page to see the hyperlink in action.

> See the *Creating hyperlinks and anchors* tutorial on p. 53 and search *Adding hyperlinks and actions* in WebPlus Help for more information on hyperlinks.

To preview the lightbox effect:

1. Preview the site in a browser. See *To preview your site in a browser* on p. 8 for details.

2. Hover the mouse over the picture—the cursor changes to a hand.

3. Click to see a larger version of the picture displayed in a lightbox.

'Self-linking picture' hyperlinks help optimize site visits as only the visitors who want to see the full size picture need to download it.

ALT & TITLE text

ALT and TITLE text is important to use to ensure that your website is accessible to everyone.

- Used to describe the content and/or purpose of a picture, **ALT text** will appear in the area of your page where the picture will download.

ALT text should *not* be used for pictures which are purely decorative.

- **TITLE text** is the tooltip text that will appear when site visitors hover over the picture in their web browsers. This text is often used to show visitors that clicking the object will trigger an action. For example, opening a larger version of the picture in a new window.

To set ALT and TITLE text for a picture:

1. Select a picture and, on the context toolbar, click **Edit Properties**.

2. In the dialog, select the **ALT and TITLE** tab.

3.   Type in your chosen TITLE and ALT text in the boxes provided.

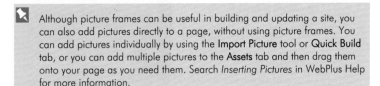

By default, the **Use default ALT text** option is selected. This tells WebPlus to use the TITLE text as the ALT description so that you only have to enter it once. By clearing the check box (as we have done above) you can have different ALT and TITLE text. You can also choose to only have ALT text.

We suggest that you experiment with ALT and TITLE text and preview your results. ALT text is an important consideration when making your site accessible to as many people as possible, and it may even help improve your site's rankings in search engine results. See the *Search Engine Optimization* tutorial on p. 185 for more information.

That's it! In this tutorial, we've explored adding pictures to frames alongside some efficiency and quality issues, and some publishing considerations.

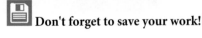

Although picture frames can be useful in building and updating a site, you can also add pictures directly to a page, without using picture frames. You can add pictures individually by using the **Import Picture** tool or **Quick Build** tab, or you can add multiple pictures to the **Assets** tab and then drag them onto your page as you need them. Search *Inserting Pictures* in WebPlus Help for more information.

Don't forget to save your work!

Creating hyperlinks and anchors

 30 min

WebPlus provides a wide and very flexible range of hyperlink options. This means easy navigation for your site's visitors—and possibly a more efficient visit if your site includes large pictures.

By the end of this tutorial you will be able to:

- Create anchors.

- Create a hyperlink to an anchor.

- Create a 'to top' hyperlink.

- Create a link to a site page.

- Create external hyperlinks.

Let's begin...

• Open the **Aperture** template as described on p. 4.

 If you have already completed the previous tutorial, you can use your saved project for this tutorial.

Introducing anchors and hyperlinks

Hyperlinks are an effective way of navigating around websites—when using the internet, you'll frequently use hyperlinks, perhaps even subconsciously.

Almost any object on your page can have a hyperlink assigned to it or can be the destination for a hyperlink. We'll explore the two most frequent examples—text and pictures.

Let's first look at setting up some page anchors.

Adding and linking to anchors

Anchors act as fixed points on your site which you can link to—anchors are used if you wish to direct visitors to a single point on a page rather than the entire page. Anchors must be created first before a hyperlink can be established to it.

Let's imagine the teaser text 'Vivamus vel' refers to the article 'Vivamus vel sapien' at the bottom of the 'Article 02' page.

First we need to add an anchor to the 'Vivamus vel sapien' article...

To add an anchor:

1. On the **Site** tab, double-click the **Article 02** page.

   Use the ↖ **Pointer Tool** to place an insertion point at the beginning of the text box next to the bottom picture frame—i.e. the words 'Vivamus vel sapien'.

   - or -

   Use the ↖ **Pointer Tool** to select the bottom picture frame.

2. On the **Properties** toolbar, click  **ID and Anchor**.

3. In the dialog, on the **ID/Anchor** tab:

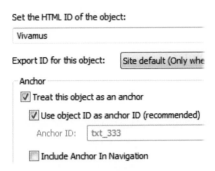

- In the **Set the HTML ID...** input box, replace the default name with something easier to remember—we used 'Vivamus'. (Names cannot contain spaces.)

- Select the **Treat this object as an anchor** option.

- Click **OK**.

Anchors can be added to any object on any page, so it's possible to create unique navigation, and to offer speedy access to any of your site's content.

Anchors for important parts of your site can be included within navigation bars by checking the **Include Anchor In Navigation** option. Make sure that you give the anchor a meaningful title as this is what your site visitors will see. See the *Navigation bars* tutorial on p. 67 for more information.

We now have an anchor which specifically identifies the article (or its picture frame) on the Article 02 page.

To make the best use of an anchor, we need to create a hyperlink to take visitors to it! Let's do this next.

To navigate to a site page:

* On the **Site** tab, double-click the **Home** page.

Locate the 'Vivamus vel' teaser text at the bottom of the page. We can use the arrow button and/or 'Lorem >>' text as links to our newly created anchor. If you select either, you will notice they have 'placeholder' hyperlinks already attached (indicated by the icon on the object's toolbar).

We'll update these to show you how to create a hyperlink to an anchor.

To link to an anchor:

1. Use the **Pointer Tool** to select the 'Lorem >>' text and click **Remove Hyperlink**.

2. With the text still selected, type 'More >>' and then drag to select the text once more.

3. On the **Properties** toolbar, click  **Hyperlink**.

4. In the dialog, on the **Hyperlink Type** tab:

- Select the **Anchor** category.

- In the **Page name** drop-down list, select **Article 02**.

- In the **Anchor** drop-down list, select the anchor name.

- Click **OK**.

The text now hyperlinks to our article anchor. However, before we preview our work, let's first modify the hyperlink on the arrow button to give visitors a navigation choice.

To modify a hyperlink:

1. Select the arrow button and then, on the object toolbar, click Hyperlink.

2. Repeat step 4 on the previous page to modify the hyperlink.

Now you have two hyperlinks to the same anchor, let's see how your site visitors can use them!

Previewing your hyperlink

It's always a good idea to test your hyperlinks to make sure they direct visitors to your intended destination. You can do this by previewing your site.

To preview a site:

1.   Preview the site in a browser. See *To preview your site in a browser* on p. 8 for details.

2.   Scroll down to either of the hyperlinked objects and hover over them. You will see the cursor change to the hand cursor.

3.   Click on either link and the Article 02 page will display with 'Vivamus vel sapien' article in full view.

As you can see, the top of the page is not visible. Currently, to return to the top of the page, a visitor needs to scroll back up. Let's help our visitors by setting up a shortcut for returning to the top of the page.

Creating 'to top' hyperlinks

For long web pages you may want to offer a link back to the top of the page. WebPlus automatically creates a 'top' anchor for every web page in your site, all you need to do is simply link text or images to this pre-defined 'top' anchor!

To create a 'top' link:

1. On the **Site** tab, double-click the **Article 02** page.

2. On the Drawing toolbar, click **A** **Artistic Text**.

3. Click at the bottom-right of the page to add a text object with default formatting.

4. Type 'Top of page' and then drag with the  **Pointer Tool** to select the text.

5. From the **Properties** menu, click **Hyperlink**.

6. In the dialog, on the **Hyperlink Type** tab:

*   Choose the **Anchor** category.

*   In the **Anchor** drop-down list, select **top**.

*   Click **OK**.

Feel free to preview your site to see the hyperlink in action.

 A 'top' link can also be added to a graphic or picture by selecting it and then follow steps 5 and 6 above.

 Save now! Click **File > Save As**.

Creating a link to a site page

Navigation bars are generally used for jumping between pages within a website. However, there may be times when you have excluded pages from the main navigation bar but still want visitors to access them easily. A hyperlink can solve this problem. See the *Navigation bars* tutorial on p. 67 for more information on navigation bars.

In our template, you can see that the Links page (among others) has been excluded from the main navigation bar.

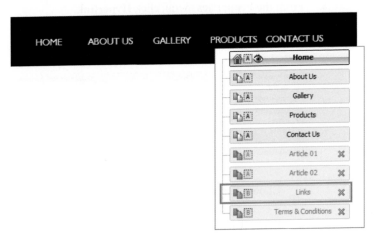

Let's create a hyperlink to the Links page and add a little flair by opening it in a lightbox.

To create a link to a site page:

1. On the **Site** tab, expand the **Master Pages** section, and then double-click on **Master A**.

Master page A will display in the workspace.

For more information on working with Master pages, search *Understanding pages and master pages* in WebPlus Help.

2. Use the **Pointer Tool** to select the 'Vestibulum' text (bottom, left of the page) and click **Remove Hyperlink**.

3. With the text still selected, type 'Links' and then drag to select the text once more.

4. From the **Properties** menu, click **Hyperlink**.

5. In the dialog:

   - On the **Hyperlink Type** tab, choose the **Site Page** category.

   - From the **Page name** drop-down list, select **Links**.

   - On the **Target Window** tab, in the **Type** drop-down list, choose **Lightbox**.

   - Click **OK**.

Feel free to preview your site to see the hyperlink in action.

You can also link from a thumbnail to a larger picture (i.e. self-linking pictures) displayed in a lightbox. See the *Framed pictures* tutorial on p. 39 for more information.

Creating an external hyperlink

For this final section, we'll look at setting up a hyperlink on the About Us page which links to an external website on the internet— the procedure is very similar to what we've previously explored throughout this tutorial.

To create an external hyperlink:

1.   On the **Site** tab, double-click the **About Us** page.

2.   Right-click the arrow button and select **Hyperlink**.

3.   In the dialog:

   •   On the **Hyperlink Type** tab, choose the **Internet Page** category.

   •   Type in the URL for the external site in the **URL address** box or click a previously entered URL from the drop-down list.

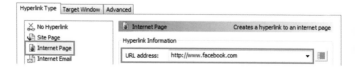

- On the **Target Window** tab, in the **Type** drop-down list, choose **New Window**.

- Click **OK**.

> Whenever linking to an external website, we recommend setting the target window or frame to **New Window**, this way your visitor will not lose access to your website—it will still be open in their browser.

Feel free to preview your site to see the hyperlink in action.

That's it! The site is now full of hyperlinks to help your visitors navigate around. We'll leave you to explore the other hyperlink types listed in the Hyperlinks dialog—most are self-explanatory.

> Hyperlinks can have a big impact on getting your website noticed by search engines. See the *Search Engine Optimization* tutorial on p.185 for more information.

> Hyperlinks and anchors can be viewed and managed from the **Site Manager**, which you can access from the context toolbar. Search *Site Manager* in WebPlus Help for more information.

Don't forget to save your work!

Navigation bars

15-20 min

Having fantastic content on your website is useless unless your
visitors can get to it! Navigation bars are essential to successful site
navigation. Luckily for us, WebPlus has a whole host of
professionally designed dynamic navigation bars for us to use, and
the process is easy.

By the end of this tutorial you will be able to:

* Change the design of an existing navigation bar.

* Add a navigation bar.

* Customize a navigation bar.

* Use Child and Same Level navigation bars.

If you're unfamiliar with website structure, we suggest you review the basic
concepts before beginning this tutorial. See the *Modifying site structure*
tutorial on p.19 and search *Understanding site structure* in WebPlus Help.

Let's begin...

• Open the **Aperture** template as described on p. 4.

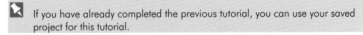
If you have already completed the previous tutorial, you can use your saved project for this tutorial.

Before we start discussing navigation bars, first let's tweak the site's structure to make site navigation a little more exciting. We'll run through this quickly as it is covered in more details in the *Modifying site structure* tutorial on p. 19.

To modify site structure:

1. On the **Site** tab, click ⊞ **Site Structure**.

2. In **Site Structure** view

   • Hold down the **Ctrl** key and then click to select the **About Us** and **Contact Us** pages.

   • Right-click the **Home** page and select **Move selected>Under this page**.

   • On the context toolbar, click ⊞ **Close Site Structure**.

The site's structure has now been modified, so let's get onto changing its navigation bar!

Save now! Click **File > Save As**.

Changing the style of an existing navigation bar

Notice that this template already contains a navigation bar.

Generally, the main '**top level**' navigation bar is shared by all of the pages on a website. As a result, the navigation bar is usually placed on the underlying master page. This means that you only have to place the navigation bar once, even though it appears on each page. Let's update the style of the navigation bar.

To change the navigation bar design:

1. ![icon] Click to select the existing navigation bar and then click **Edit on Master Page**.

The master page is displayed in the workspace.

2. Double-click the navigation bar.

3. In the **Edit Navigation Bar** dialog, select the **Type** tab.

    The category list (highlighted red) displays the available
    navigation bar categories. A preview is displayed in the main
    pane on the right.

4. Click on a category item to view a preview of the bar. (If you
    point to a part of the bar containing a pop-up menu the menu
    will also preview.) We selected the **Simple 1** navigation bar style.

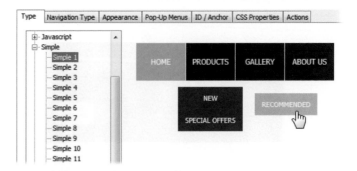

5. Click **OK**.

The navigation bar is updated on the page.

Depending on the design you chose, the navigation bar may not immediately fit correctly on the page (as with the above design). You can resize and reposition it to suit your needs.

To resize and reposition a navigation bar:

1. Click to select the navigation bar and then drag the square handles to resize the bounding box.

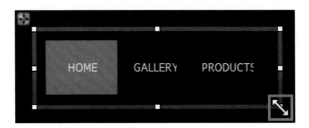

You may see a ![green exclamation mark] green exclamation mark appear if the bounding box is too small for the navigation bar. Simply drag the bounding box handles until the green exclamation mark disappears and all of the navigation bar can display correctly. You may have to do this periodically if you add more pages to your site.

2. Drag the navigation bar (using the boundary box or 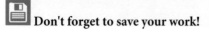 move button) into the required position. (We placed it top-right.)

Let's see how it looks by previewing the site in a web browser. See *To preview your site in a browser* on p. 8 for details.

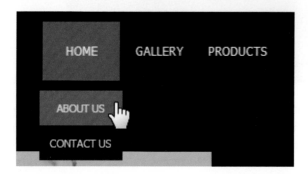

Notice that the navigation bar has updated throughout the site, even though we only changed it once. This is because it is placed on the master page.

Next we'll look at adding a new navigation bar.

> Many of the navigation bars have been created to use scheme colours and will update when placed on the page to match the current scheme. Search *Using colour schemes* in WebPlus Help for more information on using colour schemes.

Don't forget to save your work!

Adding a navigation bar

All WebPlus templates come with a navigation bar, but what if you
want to add another one (or are building a website from scratch)? A
great place to start is with Page Content assets, which include
navigation bars.

To add a navigation bar:

1. On the **Assets** tab, click the **Page Content** category header to
    display all the page content associated with the current
    template.

2. Drag the **Navbar; Horizontal** tagged asset from the **Assets** tab
    to the bottom-centre of the master page.

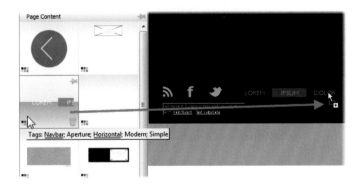

Asset tags are displayed by hovering the mouse over the asset thumbnail.

3. Resize and reposition the navigation bar neatly at the bottom-centre of the master page.

Next, we need to ensure the navigation bar always displays at the bottom of all pages using the master page, regardless of page length.

To attach an object to the bottom of a page:

• Right-click the navigation bar and then select **Arrange>Attach to Bottom of Page**.

Now we've added our navigation bar, let's see how it looks by previewing the site in a web browser.

This new navigation bar looks far from ideal. The text is aligned right and the menus drop down, almost off the screen. Let's fix this next.

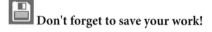 **Don't forget to save your work!**

Customizing a navigation bar

We can fix the issues mentioned above by customizing the settings of the navigation bar.

To customize the navigation bar settings:

- Select the navigation bar and then, on the context toolbar, click **Edit Navigation Bar**.

First we'll change the alignment of the buttons on the navigation bar.

To change navigation button alignment:

1. In the **Edit Navigation Bar** dialog, select the **Appearance** tab.

2. From the **Preview Background** drop-down palette, select **Black** to allow us to preview the navigation bar effectively.

3. Select the **Buttons** category from the list on the left.

4. In the **Alignment** section:

   - From the **Horizontal Alignment** drop-down list, select **Centre**.

   - From the **Vertical Alignment** drop-down list, select **Bottom**.

Next we'll ensure the menus pop up (rather than drop down).

To change menu behaviour:

1. In the **Edit Navigation Bar** dialog, on the **Pop-Up Menus** tab:

- Select the **Size and Position** category from the list on the left.

- From the **Vertical Offsets** section, from the **Position** drop-down list, select **Above**.

2. Click **OK** to exit the dialog.

Now we've customized our navigation bar, let's see how it looks by previewing the site in a web browser.

The new navigation bar looks much better now, but rather than this navigation bar replicating the information on the original, main navigation bar, let's make it do something slightly different.

Other types of navigation

In most websites, the main navigation bar is kept fairly simple, showing only the main, top-level pages of the website. However, it is not uncommon to have several types of navigation bar throughout your website. WebPlus makes this process very easy. We'll conclude this tutorial by looking at two other types of navigation, **Same Level** and **Child Level**.

The hierarchy of a site is made up of levels. These are grouped into **Top**, **Parent**, **Child** and **Same**.

Currently both of our navigation bars use the **Top Level** navigation type—i.e. they show **Home**, **Gallery** and **Products**. Instead, we'll set the lower navigation bar to a **Same Level** type.

To add a Same Level navigation type:

1. Right-click the navigation bar and select **Edit Navigation Bar**.

2. In the dialog, on the **Navigation Type** tab, click **Same Level**.

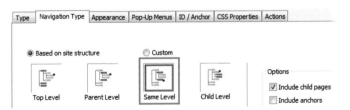

3. (Optional) To simplify the navigation bar you can remove the pop-up menus by excluding child pages—uncheck **Include child pages**.

4. Click **OK**.

Let's see how it looks by previewing the site in a web browser.

The navigation bar on the Home, Gallery and Products pages looks unchanged, this is because they are both Top Level and the Same Level. However, if you navigate to the About Us or Contact Us pages, you will see the navigation bar has updated to show the pages of the same level on their level.

Next we'll change the navigation type to Child Level and preview the effect in a browser.

To add a Child Level navigation type:

1. Right-click the navigation bar and select **Edit Navigation Bar**.

2. In the dialog, on the **Navigation Type** tab, click **Child Level**.

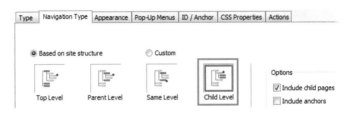

3. Click **OK**.

Let's see how it looks by previewing the site in a web browser.

The navigation bar on the Home page displays navigation to its child pages, About Us and Contact Us, while all other pages do not have a navigation bar because they have no child pages.

The Same and Child Level types of navigation allow visitors to get to relevant pages on the site, without delving through menus. It also makes it obvious that there is more content to see.

That's it! We've now got to the end of this tutorial. However, we've only just scratched the surface of all the things you can do with navigation bars. Search *Inserting navigation bars* in WebPlus Help for more inspiration.

 Don't forget to save your work!

Object styles

15 min

The Styles tab contains pre-defined object styles which you can quickly apply to text and objects to create dramatic effects. In this tutorial, we'll look at enhancing a web page using object styles.

By the end of this tutorial you will be able to:

- Add a new page from the Asset Browser.

- Apply single object styles.

- Apply multiple object styles.

- Modify object styles.

Let's begin...

* Open the **Aperture** template as described on p. 4.

 If you have already completed the previous tutorial, you can use your saved project for this tutorial.

Adding a new page

We'll demonstrate using object styles on a page layout found in the Tutorials assets pack.

To add a new template page:

1. On the **Site** tab, click the down arrow next to ▾ **Add new page or link** and select **New Template Page**.

    The Asset Browser will open in the workspace.

2. In the **Pack Files** section on the left, select the **Tutorials** pack.

3. In the **Tutorials** gallery, select the **object styles** tagged page.

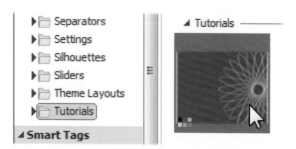

4. Click **OK**.

The new page will be displayed in the workspace, and selected in the **Site** tab.

 Feel free to rename the new page, but for the purposes of this tutorial we'll leave it as the default.

 Save now! Click **File** > **Save As**.

Using the Styles tab

The **Styles** tab contains a variety of object styles (saved attributes or properties such as line colour, fill, reflections and shadows) that can be applied to objects with a single click.

To apply a style to an object:

1. From the **Basic** toolbar, select the **Pointer Tool**, and then click the rectangle at the top of the page.

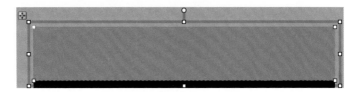

2.   On the **Styles** tab:

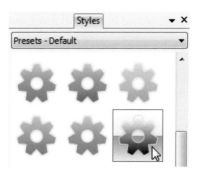

- From the category drop-down list, select **Presets - Default**.

- Click the **Default 12** thumbnail to apply it to the rectangle.

The Default 12 object style consists of a gradient fill, line colour and style, and a drop shadow. These attributes are automatically applied to the rectangle.

Repeat the above steps to apply the same style to the bottom rectangle.

Object styles can just as easily be applied to Artistic text!

To apply an object style to Artistic text:

1. From the **Basic** toolbar, select the  **Pointer Tool**, and then click 'Vivamus'.

2. On the **Styles** tab:

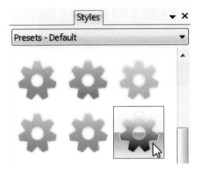

   - From the category drop-down list, select **Presets - Default**.

   - Click the **Default 12** thumbnail.

The Default 12 object style attributes are automatically applied to the Artistic text.

Frame text acts differently to Artistic text. Object styles are applied to the text frame only, rather than the text inside it.

To apply a style to a text frame:

1. From the **Basic** toolbar, select the  **Pointer Tool**.

2. Click on the title text, and then click to select the text's frame (the border turns solid).

3. On the **Styles** tab:

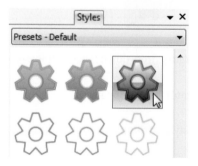

    • From the category drop-down list, select **Presets - Default**.

    • Click the **Default 25** thumbnail.

The Default 25 object style attributes are automatically applied to the text frame.

The colour of the text within the frame has updated, but it hasn't taken on the gradient style. This is because it is HTML text and only supports the use of solid fills. (See the *Frame text* tutorial on p. 29 for more information on frame text.)

You don't have to feel restricted to applying just one object style. In WebPlus, it's really easy to apply multiple object styles to a single object.

Applying multiple styles

 You can apply more than one style to an object at any point during your design process. The styles will complement rather than replace each other. This means you can 'stack up' object styles on one object to achieve your desired effect.

 When selecting an object style from the **Presets** (Default, Fun, and Materials) categories, the style may replace attributes already applied to the object. This is because the Presets category styles are designed using a variety of attributes. Furthermore, the **3D** category styles do not support some other attributes.

To apply multiple styles:

1. From the **Basic** toolbar, select the 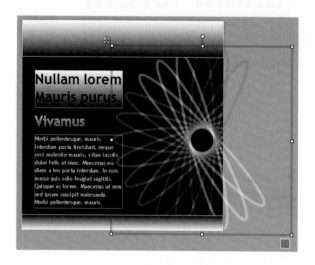 **Pointer Tool** and then click the spiral graphic.

2. On the **Styles** tab:

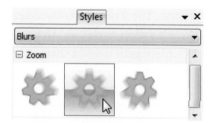

- From the category drop-down list, select **Blurs**.

- Click the **Zoom 02** thumbnail.

The spiral graphic has become blurred.

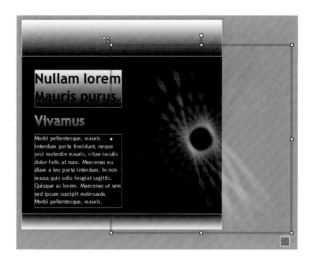

Let's add another effect.

3. Again, on the **Styles** tab:

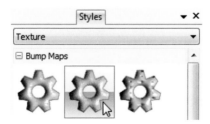

- From the category drop-down list, select **Texture**.

- Click the **Texture 05** thumbnail.

The texture style is added to the object, complementing the blur style previously applied.

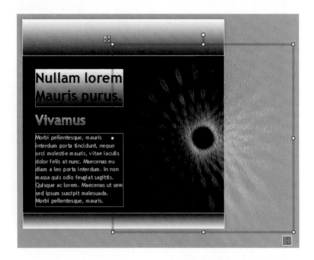

Our web page is almost complete. However, before we leave, let's have a look at another powerful feature of object styles—modifying an object style.

 Don't forget to save your work!

Modifying object styles

When you modify an object style, any object in your website which shares that style will update accordingly. This is a quick but effective way of changing the design of your website while maintaining consistency.

To modify object styles:

1. On the **Styles** tab:

    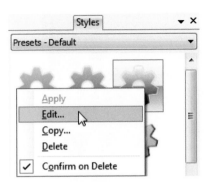

    *   From the category drop-down list, select **Presets - Default**.

    *   Right-click the **Default 12** thumbnail and select **Edit**.

2. In the **Style Attributes Editor** dialog, in the **General** category, double-click **Line Style**.

    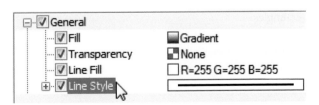

3. In the **Line and Border** dialog, increase the weight of the line to **5 pix**.

4. Click **OK** twice to exit both dialogs.

The outlines of both the top and bottom rectangles have become more prominent.

You will see that the outline of the artistic text has also become more prominent, because it shares the same style as the top and bottom rectangles.

That's it! We hope you've enjoyed exploring the Styles tab, and learning how object styles can be used to enhance your designs. Search *Using object styles* in WebPlus Help for more information about object styles.

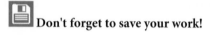 **Don't forget to save your work!**

Floating panels

20 min

Panels have special properties which mean that they can be free-floating, remain in view even when the window is scrolled and have actions assigned to them. It makes the panel a really useful tool. In this tutorial we'll look at creating a floating panel.

By the end of this tutorial you will be able to:

* Attach a floating panel to a browser window.

* Position a floating panel effectively.

* Understand how object order affects floating panels.

Let's begin...

*   Open the **Aperture** template as described on p. 4.

 If you have already completed the previous tutorial, you can use your saved project for this tutorial.

Floating panels

A panel can become a 'floating' object that is permanently attached to the browser window. This means it won't scroll with the page. It can be used to permanently display a navigation bar, either at the side or top of the window, or for advertising. We'll look at the latter purpose.

To add a panel to a page:

1. On the **Assets** tab, click the **Page Content** category header to display all the page content associated with the current template.

2. Drag the **1 Column; Panel** tagged asset from the **Assets** tab onto the page, and position it on the right, just below the navigation bar.

Asset tags are displayed by hovering the mouse over the asset thumbnail.

The panel is added to the page and, by default, scrolls with the page.

Save now! Click **File** > **Save As**.

Let's see how it looks by previewing the site in a web browser. See *To preview your site in a browser* on p. 8 for details.

Notice as you scroll that the panel scrolls with the page and is not visible once you reach the bottom of the page.

Next we'll update the panel's settings so it appears permanently at
the top right.

To attach panel to a browser window:

1. 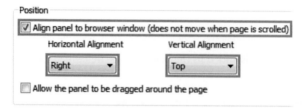 Click to select the panel, then on the context toolbar, click
   Edit Panel.

2. In the dialog:

   Position
   ☑ Align panel to browser window (does not move when page is scrolled)

   Horizontal Alignment   Vertical Alignment

   | Right ▾ | | Top ▾ |

   ☐ Allow the panel to be dragged around the page

   - Select **Align panel to browser window**.

   - From the **Horizontal Alignment** drop-down list, select
     Right.

   - From the **Vertical Alignment** drop-down list, select **Top**.

   - Click **OK**.

Now we've updated the panel settings, let's see how it looks by previewing the site in a web browser.

The panel is now fixed to the side of the browser window, appearing to float above the website. It stays in position when the page scrolls.

Depending on the width of the browser window, you may also notice the panel move further to the right. We'll discuss the reason for this next.

Positioning of floating panels

Once a panel is aligned to the browser window, it no longer has an absolute position. Instead, the panel has a relative position which is determined by its position on the page and horizontal and vertical alignment settings.

The position of the panel on the page is used to offset the panel position in the browser, e.g. a panel aligned horizontally left and 10 pixels from the left edge of the page will be positioned 10 pixels from the left edge of your browser window.

To find the optimum position for your floating panel, we recommend using the Align tab to replicate the panel's alignment attachment settings. You can then adjust the position of the panel between previews to get the position perfect.

Let's do this now.

To update a floating panel's alignment:

1.   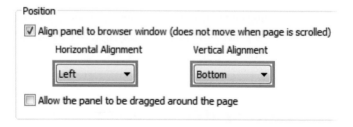 Click to select the panel, then on the context toolbar, click **Edit Panel**.

2.   In the dialog:

    Position
    ☑ Align panel to browser window (does not move when page is scrolled)

    Horizontal Alignment   Vertical Alignment

    | Left   ▼ | | Bottom   ▼ |

    ☐ Allow the panel to be dragged around the page

    - From the **Horizontal Alignment** drop-down list, select **Left**.

    - From the **Vertical Alignment** drop-down list, select **Bottom**.

    - Click **OK**.

3.   With the panel still selected, on the **Align** tab:

*   From the **Relative to** drop-down list, selected **Page**.

*   Click  **Left** and **Bottom**.

Now we've updated the panel settings and aligned it according to those settings, let's see how it looks by previewing the site in a web browser.

The panel stays attached to the bottom left of the browser window regardless of scrolling or window resizing. However, when reaching the bottom of the page, the panel overlaps the footer. We can ensure this does not happen by repositioning the panel on the page and therefore its relative position in the browser window.

To move a panel (and its relative floating position):

- Hold down the **Shift** key and drag the panel upwards until the footer is visible.

Now we've updated the panel's position, let's see how it looks by previewing the site in a web browser.

The panel no longer covers the footer when scrolling to the bottom of the page. You will also notice it maintains a constant gap with the bottom of the browser window whenever the page is scrolled. This is the same gap distance between the panel and the bottom of the page in WebPlus.

Floating panels and object order (z-order)

If you add any page content after adding your floating panel, you might find on previewing that the panel scrolls **underneath** the new page content.

This is because floating panels are still affected by z-order (the stacking of objects on the page). This can be easily rectified by ensuring the panel is the highest in the z-order before previewing and publishing your site.

To bring the panel to the top of the z-order:

* Select the panel and, on the **Arrange** toolbar, click 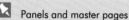 **Bring to Front**.

That's it! You've now created a floating panel and know how to position it effectively.

 Panels and master pages

You can add a floating panel to any master page, so it displays on all pages using that master page. This is useful if your panel includes some form of advertising or navigation which you wish displayed throughout your site.

However, if you do add a floating panel to a master page, you need to remember to adjust the order of the master page in the Objects tab. To do this, display the Objects tab and then drag the master page containing your floating panel (Master C in this example) to the top of the stack.

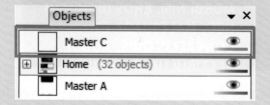

All objects placed on the master page (Master C in this example) will now display on top of your content. You will need to do this for each page that uses the master page. Search *Understanding pages and master pages* in WebPlus Help for more information on using master pages.

Don't forget to save your work!

Sliders

 30 min

If you want to really add some style to your website, then you might want to consider using sliders. Sliders allow you to create a wide variety of subtle animated elements on your website, from banners and advertisements to photo galleries and even for navigation!

By the end of this tutorial you will be able to:

• Identify and select an existing slider on a page.

• View alternative slider panels.

• Modify slider content.

• Modify slider animation.

• Add a slider to your page.

Let's begin...

* Open the **Aperture** template as described on p. 4.

 If you have already completed the previous tutorial, you can use your saved project for this tutorial.

What are sliders?

Sliders are essentially animated panels. They get their name from the most commonly used animation effect which uses a slide transition effect from one slider panel to the next. Sliders are often used to simply display different images in a similar way to a photo gallery, but they can also be used to create elements such as animated banners, great looking navigation elements, and news items. In fact, sliders can even be programmed to display certain panels on a specific date, meaning that they can make a great tool for creating advertisements or for highlighting a special event.

The theme layout that we've opened has three pages that contain sliders—the Home, About Us, and Products pages. We'll look at the slider on the Home page first.

Let's see how it looks by previewing the site in a web browser. See *To preview your site in a browser* on p. 8 for details.

On the Home page, you'll see that clicking the arrow on the left or right of the slider alternates a set of three panels by scrolling them from the left.

Identifying and selecting sliders

Sliders come in many forms and all of the ones available in WebPlus can be customized to suit your needs. The slider on the Home page is one of the more simple types. We'll start by customizing this and then have a look at some of the other sliders available.

If a slider contains pictures, and is placed on the page with other pictures, it can be hard to tell at first glance where the sliders are. The easiest way to identify and then select your sliders is by using the **Objects** tab.

To identify and select an existing slider:

1. On the **Objects** tab:

    •   Click the small + to expand the Home page objects.

    •   From the **Show** drop-down list, select **Slider**.

        Only sliders on the page are displayed in the Objects tab.

2. Click on the slider object in the **Objects** tab.

On the page, you can see that the slider panel has been selected. Note the slider controls at the bottom of the slider.

Also notice the context toolbar at the top of the workspace updates.

So, how do you access the other panels you could see when previewing the site template? We'll show you this next.

To view alternative panels on a slider:

1. With the slider selected, click once on the  **Show Next Panel** button. A second panel is displayed.

Alternatively, you can select a specific panel...

2. On the context toolbar, from the panel drop-down list, select **Foreground**. Notice that this panel is blank.

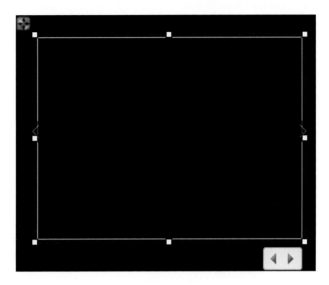

This is a foreground panel. Anything placed on this panel will appear on top of all of the other panels as they're displayed. We'll look at this in more detail in the *Foreground slider panels* section on p. 115.

Finally, you can select specific panels using the Objects tab.

3. On the **Objects** tab:

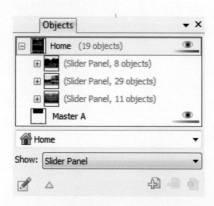

*   From the **Show** drop-down list, select **Slider foreground** or **Slider Panel** to list the foreground panel or all other panels in the tab, respectively.

*   Clicking on any of the entries in the tab will select that panel on the slider.

Now we've looked at selecting sliders and individual slider panels, let's look at how they can be modified!

Modifying slider content

Sliders can contain virtually any type of content that could be placed on the page. The professionally designed sliders included with WebPlus primarily contain pictures, shapes or text. The pictures are placed within a frame which means that they can easily be replaced with your own content. Let's do this now.

(For more information on working with text and pictures, see the *Frame text* and *Framed pictures* tutorials on p. 29 and 39, respectively.)

First of all, we'll import the tutorial pictures into the **Assets** tab. However, you can use your own pictures if you want to.

To add Picture assets to the Assets tab:

1. On the **Assets** tab, click 📁 **Browse** to open the **Asset Browser**.

2. In the **Categories** section, click to select the **Pictures** category. The pictures from all installed packs are displayed in the main pane.

3. In the main pane the assets are categorized by the Pack file that they belong to. In the **Tutorials** pack, click **Add All** ✅.

    The green ✅ shows that the assets have been added to the tab.

4. Click **Close** to exit.

Now that we've imported our picture assets, we can add them to the frames on the slider.

To change a picture on a slider panel:

1. Select the slider and then, on the context toolbar, from the panel drop-down list, select **3: Panel**.

2. On the **Objects** tab, from the **Show** drop-down list, select **Slider Panel** and then click **Slider Panel, 8 objects**.

3. Click once on the picture.

The picture frame controls are now displayed instead of the slider controls. This is because the picture is now selected and not the slider.

4. Drag a picture from the **Assets** tab onto the slider. The current picture will be highlighted to show that it will be replaced.

5. On release, the picture is replaced.

We'll repeat the process to replace another picture.

To select a slider panel and change its contents:

1. From the **Edit** menu, click **Select > Select Parent** (or press **Ctrl+R**) to select the slider panel.

    With the slider panel selected, the context toolbar updates at the top of the workspace.

Pressing **Ctrl+R** also works when dealing with panels and forms.

2. With the panel selected, click **Show Next Panel** twice.

3. Click once on the picture and then drag another picture from the **Assets** tab onto the slider.

4. Click inside the 'VIVAMUS VEL SAPIEN' text frame and press **Ctrl+A** to select all the text.

5. Type a new title, e.g. 'EXPLORE THE GROUNDS'.

Now we've updated our slider panels, let's see how it looks by previewing the site in a web browser.

Next, we'll edit the foreground panel and see how this effects our slider.

 Save now! Click **File** > **Save As**.

Foreground slider panels

To explore the uses of the foreground slider panel, we'll use the slider on the About Us page.

To navigate between pages:

• On the **Site** tab, double-click **About Us** to open the page in the workspace.

We'll add a button to the foreground slider panel so it appears on all of the slider panels.

To edit the foreground panel:

1. On the **Objects** tab, expand the **Slider, 4 objects** entry and then select **Slider foreground**.

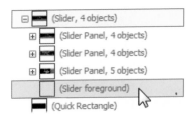

    The foreground panel is displayed. Now we can add our content directly to it.

2. On the **Assets** tab, click the **Page Content** category header to display all the page content associated with the current template.

3. Drag the **Lorem** button from the **Assets** tab onto the slider panel, and position it on the top left.

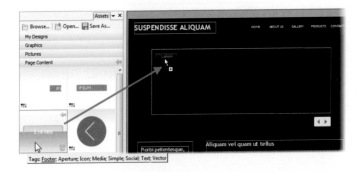

Asset tags are displayed by hovering the mouse over the asset thumbnail.

Now we've updated our foreground slider panel, let's see how it looks by previewing the site in a web browser.

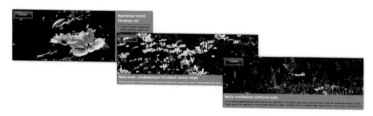

The foreground panel is a great place to put information that you always want people to see. Examples of its use could be for contact information, a button or a watermark. As the foreground panel itself cannot be animated, you could add a picture to it. This way you can use a single image with animated text panels. You'll find examples of different kinds of sliders in the **Asset Browser**.

Modifying slider animation

As well as amending slider content, it's also easy to change the animation style. We'll look at this now.

To edit slider animation type:

1. Using the **Objects** tab, select the slider.

2. On the slider context toolbar, click ![icon] **Edit Slider**.

   The **Edit Slider** dialog opens. From here we can change the animation style, timing and whether or not it loops continuously.

3. On the **Options** tab:

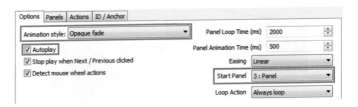

- In the **Animation style:** drop-down list, click **Opaque fade**.

- Select **Autoplay**.

- In the **Start Panel** drop-down list, select **3 : Panel**.

- Click **OK** to exit the dialog.

Now we've updated our slider animation, let's see how it looks by previewing the site in a web browser.

You will notice that the slider now displays the third panel first then automatically cycles through the panels (Autoplay). The animation has changed to a subtle fade (Opaque fade). Clicking one of the arrow buttons will stop the slider automatically cycling through the panels—you can change this by unchecking **Stop play when Next / Previous clicked** option in the **Edit Slider** dialog.

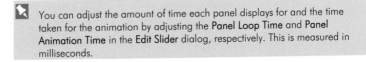

You can adjust the amount of time each panel displays for and the time taken for the animation by adjusting the **Panel Loop Time** and **Panel Animation Time** in the **Edit Slider** dialog, respectively. This is measured in milliseconds.

Adding a slider to a page

If you want to add a new slider to your site, you'll find many different types of slider in the **Assets Browser** ready to be added to your page and customized to suit your requirements.

To add sliders to the Assets tab:

1. On the **Assets** tab, click ⬜ **Browse** to open the **Asset Browser**.

2. In the **Categories** section, select the **Page Content** category and then in the search box type 'slider'.

3. From the Page Content gallery, click to select individual sliders or click the **Add All** ✅ button to add an entire pack.

   The green ✅ shows the asset(s) will be added to the **Assets** tab.

4. Click **Close** to exit the dialog and return to the page.

   The sliders are displayed in the **Assets** tab.

Next we'll add one of these sliders to the page.

To add a slider to the page:

1. On the **Assets** tab, the **Page Content** category should be displayed (if not, click the header).

2. Drag any slider onto the page.

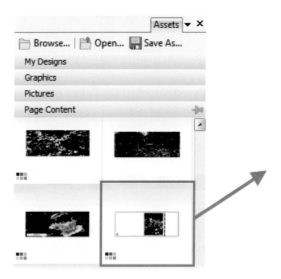

That's it! As you can see, sliders are extremely useful objects. When added to your page, they not only make the page look good, but they can also add a lot of functionality. Have fun!

 We've looked at sliders which contain mainly images. However, you'll find more fully customizable sliders of all styles in the **Asset Browser**. We recommend that you spend some time familiarising yourself with these sliders as you're bound to find one that's suitable for your needs.

 Don't forget to save your work!

Serif Web Resources

5 min

Serif owns and operates a secure server space, called **Serif Web Resources**, which is available to all customers for managing a range of WebPlus Smart objects (e.g., forums, blogs, accommodation booker, access control, mailing lists, and more). Serif Web Resources can also be used to securely collect data from your website forms. To access Serif Web Resources, you will need to create a Serif Web Resources account. We'll show you how to sign up to an account.

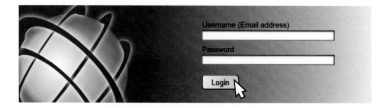

By the end of this tutorial you will be able to:

- Create a new Serif Web Resources account.

- Access an existing account.

Let's begin...

You can create a Serif Web Resources account through WebPlus.

> Even if you have multiple websites, you only need one Serif Web Resources account to manage the Smart objects across all your websites.

To create a Serif Web Resources account:

1. Open an existing WebPlus project or, from the **File** menu, select **New**.

2. From the **Insert** menu, select **Smart Object**.

3. In the login dialog, click **Create Account**.

Username (Email address)

Password

Login   ☑ Remember account details

Create Account   Forgotten Password?

4. In the next dialog:

    *   In the **Username** input box, type the email address you want to link to your Serif Web Resources account. Then retype this in the **Confirm Email** input box.

    *   In the **Screen name** input box, type a personalized screen name.

- In the **Choose a password** input box, type a password and then retype it in the **Retype the password** input box.

- Click **Terms And Conditions** to launch and read the Serif Web Resources Terms and Conditions. If you agree to the Terms and Conditions, return to WebPlus and select the **Check this box if you agree...** option.

- Click **Signup**.

> If your email address is not already associated with a Serif account, you will be asked to provide a few extra details. Follow the instructions in the dialog.

A confirmation email is sent to your email address. Click the link in the email and you're ready to access Serif Web Resources!

> If you don't receive an email, be sure to check your Spam folder!

Accessing Serif Web Resources

Once you have created your Serif Web Resources account, you can access it through WebPlus or directly from the internet (http://www.serifwebresources.com).

To access Serif Web Resources:

1. In WebPlus, from the **Tools** menu, click **Serif Web Resources**.

   Your default browser will open the Serif Web Resources login page.

2. On the login page:

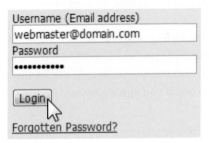

- Type your username (email address).

- Type your password.

- Click **Login**.

Your Serif Web Resources account will open where you can manage your account (click **My Account**) and Smart objects settings.

> You can also access your Serif Web Resources account via **Insert>Smart objects**, where you can optionally store your account details for automatic logging in.

That's it! You have created and accessed your Serif Web Resources account.

You can use this account to create and manage a range of powerful and popular web features. These objects don't require any programming expertise to set up, so using them to add interactive content is within the capabilities of every WebPlus user. Search *Using Smart objects* in WebPlus Help for more information on adding Smart objects.

You can also use your Serif Web Resources account to collect data from your website forms. See the following tutorial, *Competition forms*, for more information.

Manage your smart objects from anywhere!

Once you start using smart objects (blogs, forums, accommodation booker, etc.), you'll probably want to update them on a regular basis. In this case, you'll be interested to know that you don't need your copy of WebPlus open in front of you to do it! All you need is a computer with access to the internet.

To manage your smart objects online, go to www.serifwebresources.com and log in. You'll be able to edit and manage many of your smart objects from the Smart Objects Library.

Competition forms

 30 min

Web-based forms are useful tools. In this tutorial, we're going to add a competition form to our site to allow site visitors to participate in an online competition.

By the end of this tutorial you will be able to:

• Create a form using Form Designer.

• Update a form using Form Designer including field validation.

• Set up form submission using Serif Web Resources.

• Add a reCAPTCHA™ field.

• Customize a form on the page.

This tutorial assumes that you have already registered for a **Serif Web Resources** account. If you are unsure how to do this, see the *Serif Web Resources* tutorial on p. 121.

Let's begin...

• Open the **Aperture** template as described on p. 4.

 If you have already completed the previous tutorial, you can use your saved project for this tutorial.

Adding a form

Forms can be used to collect a variety of data from site visitors. Data collected can be as simple as the person's name and email address, or a whole host of personal information. How much data you ask for on a form really depends on what you need it for.

First, let's add a new page to host our form.

To add a form to the page:

1. On the **Site** tab, double-click **Article 02** to open the page in the workspace.

2. On the **Assets** tab:

   • Click the **Pages** category header to display all the pages associated with the current template.

- Drag the **Terms & Conditions** tagged page to the right of the current page.

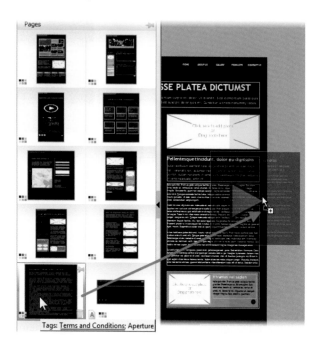

When an arrow appears pointing to the right, release the mouse button to place the page.

Asset tags are displayed by hovering the mouse over the asset thumbnail.

3. Click on a blank area of the page and then press **Ctrl+A** to select all page content.

4. Press the **Delete** key to delete all page content.

5. On the **Quick Build** tab, in the **Forms** category, drag the **Form** item onto the blank page.

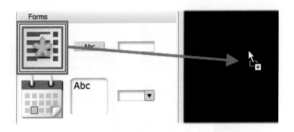

The Form Designer dialog opens.

Now we'll use Form Designer to create our competition form.

 The form will be added to the page on exiting **Form Designer** by clicking OK.

Creating a form using Form Designer

Form Designer comes complete with a range of templates to help you quickly create a variety of forms. We'll select a form template and then customize it to suit the scenario of a competition form.

 There is a competition form preset available in Form Designer but to enhance the learning experience we'll use another preset as our starting point.

To create a form:

1. On the **Templates** tab, select **Multiple - Radio Buttons** from the list of **Form Templates**.

A preview of the form can be seen on the right of the dialog.

2. On the **Theme** tab, select the design listed under **Assets Tab**.

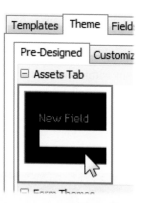

The form adopts the scheme of the Aperture theme layout and the preview updates to show the changes.

Our form looks excellent, but currently uses placeholder options. Next we'll look at some of the various ways you can update the form.

Updating a pre-designed form

There's a whole range of ways you can edit your pre-designed form within Form Designer. We're going to walk you through a few modifications you may wish to make.

First, let's update the form to create a competition with two answer options: True and False.

To update field names:

1. Select the **Fields** tab and then move your cursor over the form preview.

    As your cursor moves, sections within the form are highlighted. The preview has become interactive, allowing you to update various areas of the form.

2. Click to select **Option 1**.

3. On the **Field Properties** tab:

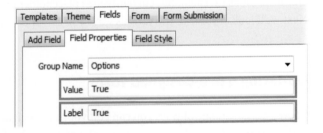

    *   In the **Value** input box, drag to highlight the default text and type 'True'.

    *   Repeat the above procedure for the **Label** input box.

4. In the preview, click to select **Option 2** and then update the **Value** and **Label** field properties to 'False'.

5. ☒ In the preview, click to select **Option 3** and then click **Delete**.

6. Repeat the above step to delete **Option 4**.

7. In the preview, click to select the **Submit** button and, on the **Field Properties** tab, in the **Label** input box, drag to highlight the default text and type 'Enter now!'.

The preview will update as you make your changes.

So we can contact the competition winner, we can make it mandatory for the Email field to be completed before the form can be submitted.

To add field validation:

1. In the preview, click to select the **Email** text box and then select the **Field Validation** tab.

2. Select the **Required...** option and then type a message into the **Message** box which will appear if the visitor attempts to submit the form without completing the field.

The preview will update to add **(required)** to the Email field to show visitors they must fill the field in.

Next, we'll update the form name, to help you identify it, and the form title, which is shown on the form.

To update the form title:

- On the **Form** tab:

- In the **Form Name** input box, drag to highlight the default text and type 'Competition Form'.

- In the **Form Title** input box, drag to highlight the default text and type 'Monthly Competition'.

The preview will update as you make your changes and should now resemble the illustration below.

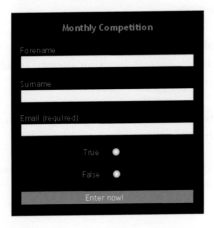

Now we have the form fields set up ready for visitors to fill out, we need to include standard text to introduce the competition, present the question, and explain about terms and conditions. We'll demonstrate this now...

To add text fields to a form:

1. Clik to select the **Fields** tab.

2. Select the **Add Field** tab and then, from the **Advanced** category, click **Text Label**.

3. In the preview, click to select the new Text Label field.

4. On the **Field Properties** tab, in the **Label** input box, type the question for your form.

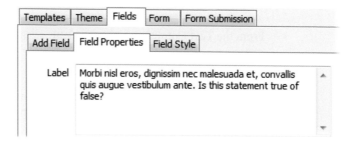

5. On the **Field Style** tab:

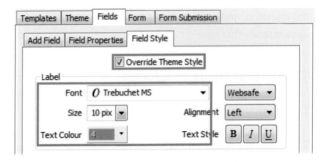

- Select the **Override Theme** style option.

- In the Label section, from the **Font** drop-down list, select **Trebuchet MS**.

- From the **Size** drop-down list, select **10 pix**.

- From the **Text Colour** drop-down palette, select **Scheme Colour 4**.

6. In the preview, click to select the **Text Label** field and then click **Move Up** until the question is placed just above the True/False radio button options.

7. If required, repeat steps 1-5 to add an introduction to your competition, placing it under the form title.

8. Repeat steps 1-5 again to add your terms and conditions before the Enter now! button—you may wish to set the text **Alignment** to **Centre** from the **Field Style** tab.

Let's see what our form looks like on our web page.

To exit Form Designer:

1. In the dialog, click **OK**.

2. You will receive a warning that no action has been set to the form. We will discuss this later, so for now, click **OK**.

   Your form is added to the page.

Next we'll look at setting a submission action to the form so when visitors complete it, the information is sent to you (as the webmaster).

 Save now! Click **File > Save As**.

Form submission via Serif Web Resources

We recommend using Serif Web Resources as the destination for data submission. Serif Web Resources will collect the data and then send it to a specified email address.

To use Serif Web Resources to collect data:

1. Select the form and, on the context toolbar, click **Form Designer**.

   The Form Designer dialog opens.

2. On the **Form Submission** tab:

   - Select **Serif Web Resources**.

   - Next to the **Email Address** field, click **Select**.

3. In the **Form Email Targets** dialog, select the email address linked to your **Serif Web Resources** account.

 If you want to add a new email target address, you'll need to add this in the **New Target** section. You'll also need to confirm the email address via the confirmation email before you can receive form submissions to it.

4. Click **Edit**.

5. Type a subject for your form dialog and then type a confirmation message that the user will see when they submit the form.

When you're ready, click **Update**.

Your change will be displayed in the **Available Email Targets** section.

6. Click **OK** twice to exit both dialogs and return to the WebPlus workspace.

We have now set the form submission via Serif Web Resources. This means that when a visitor fills in the form, the data is sent via Serif Web Resources to the email address selected.

To protect yourself from receiving spam from your form, you can use CAPTCHA or reCAPTCHA™. As you have used Serif Web Resources as the form submission, you now have two choices:

- If your form does not include a CAPTCHA or reCAPTCHA™ field, Serif Web Resources will automatically redirect visitors to a page where they will need to complete a reCAPTCHA™ field before the data from the form is submitted. If you are happy with this, you can skip to *Resizing the page* on p. 144.

- Alternatively, you can add your own CAPTCHA or reCAPTCHA™ field to the bottom of the form. We'll show how to add a reCAPTCHA™ field next.

 Don't forget to save your work!

Adding a reCAPTCHA™ field

It is useful to include a reCAPTCHA™ field on your form to help prevent spam being sent to your email address. We'll show you how to add one to your form.

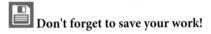 To use a reCAPTCHA™ field on your own website, you will need a valid Google account.

To add a reCAPTCHA field:

1. Double-click the form to access **Form Designer**.

2. On the **Fields** tab, in the **Advanced** category, select **reCAPTCHA™**.

   The preview will update to add the new field.

   We'll move this above the **Enter now!** button to make filling out the form more logical.

3.  In the preview, click to select the **reCAPTCHA™** field and then click **Move Up**.

You will need public and private reCAPTCHA™ keys to continue with the set up process—for this you will need an active Google account. We'll look at this next.

To generate public and private reCAPTCHA™ keys:

1. In the preview, click to select the **reCAPTCHA™** field and then select the **Field Properties** tab.

2. Click **Get reCAPTCHA™ Keys**.

3. On the Google login page, sign into or create a new Google account.

4. In the **Domain** field, type your website address and then click **Create Key**.

   You will be presented with a public and private key.

Leave the browser open for the moment so you can transfer the keys to WebPlus.

To add reCAPTCHA™ keys to WebPlus:

1. In the browser, drag to select the public key code and then copy the text by pressing **Ctrl+C**.

2. Return to WebPlus and click in the **Public Key** input box and paste in the code by pressing **Ctrl+V**.

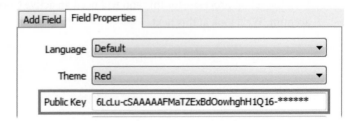

3. Repeat steps 1 and 2, to add the **Private Key** code to Form Designer.

4. Click **OK**.

Your form, complete with reCAPTCHA™, is updated on the page.

The form looks excellent, however, it extends beyond the end of the page. We'll fix this next.

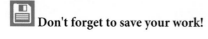 **Don't forget to save your work!**

Resizing the page

Depending on the length of the text you included in the Text Label fields, you may need to resize your page to accommodate your form. We'll show you how.

To resize the page:

1. From the **Basic** toolbar, select the ↖ **Pointer Tool**.

2. Hover the cursor at the bottom of the page until it changes to show a double-headed arrow.

3. Click and drag downwards to increase the height (length) of the page until the form fits on the page neatly.

Why not preview your site in the browser and test the form? See *To preview your site in a browser* on p. 8 for details.

If you fill out the form and then click **Enter now!** to submit the form, you should receive an email with details which look similar to the illustration below.

Serif Web Resources <server@serifwebresources.com>

to me ▾

Name_name_1: Serif
Name_name_2: Nottingham
Email: serif@webplus.net
Options: True
Submit: Enter now!

That's it! You've created a competition form for your website. The tools used in this tutorial are not limited to creating just a competition form, you can create any type of form—contact, sign in, surveys and polls, and many more.

 There is a contact form located on the **Contact Us** page which you might want to investigate, modify and customize to suit your needs.

 Don't forget to save your work!

Other things to consider

When creating your forms there are other things you may wish to consider, and we'll briefly discuss them here.

Change your reCAPTCHA™ colour scheme

The default red reCAPTCHA™ colour may not work with your site's colour scheme. This can be changed in Form Designer or the Edit Form reCAPTCHA™ dialog. In the **Theme** drop-down list, select from **Red**, **White**, **Black Glass**, or **Clean**.

Linking to Terms and Conditions

It's a good idea for certain forms (such as competition forms) to include terms and conditions. However, adding these to the bottom of a form can make the form lengthy and unreadable. Instead, you can provide a link to your terms and conditions page, which might provide a bookmarked section regarding competitions.

 To add a hyperlink to the text, you will need to unlock the form. Select the form and then, on the context toolbar, click **Unlock Form**.

By unlocking the form you will no longer be able to use Form Designer to edit the fields in your form. However, you will still be able to edit each form field by right-clicking it and selecting **Edit**.

Displaying forms

In this tutorial, we created a form on a new blank page. This page can be renamed and excluded from navigation bars (from the **Properties** menu, select **Page Properties**). The page may then be accessed via hyperlinks from other pages, perhaps opening in a lightbox.

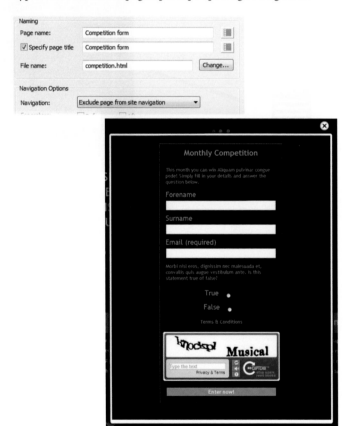

Alternatively, you may wish to add your form to an existing page (see the contact form on the **Contact Us** page).

Save a custom form

Once you have perfected your custom form, you can add it to the
Page Content category in the **Assets** tab for later use.

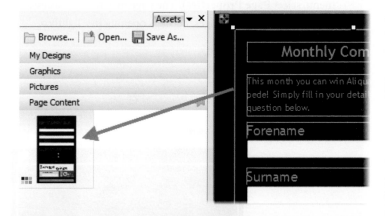

 If you wish to use this form design on a different WebPlus site, you'll need to add the form to the **My Designs** category of the Assets tab or save the design to an Assets pack. Search *Storing custom assets and asset settings* and *Creating custom Asset Packs* in WebPlus Help for more information.

Don't forget to save your work!

Making your website mobile-ready

 40 min

Optimizing your website for viewing on a mobile device is straightforward. The process involves adding pages with a mobile-specific width, modifying appropriate navigation bars, and setting up automatic redirection between pages within your website.

By the end of this tutorial you will be able to:

• Add mobile template pages to your site.

• Modify Master page navigation bars.

• Set up page redirects.

• Create mobile pages based on other site pages.

> We're going to use the Aperture theme layout in this tutorial. However, you can undertake the steps outlined with your own site, although you may wish to create mobile pages based on your site pages (see below) before proceeding.

Let's begin...

• Open the **Aperture** template as described on p. 4.

> If you have already completed the previous tutorial, you can use your saved
> project for this tutorial.

The first step to making our site mobile-ready is to create some pages which will display well on mobile devices. When adding mobile pages to your site, you can either add pre-designed mobile template pages (see below) or create mobile pages based on other site pages (see p. 167).

Adding mobile template pages

WebPlus comes complete with two pre-designed mobile template pages for each Pro Design Template and Theme Layout design. These are located in Asset packs and can be added to the Assets tab. To keep the look of our site consistent, we'll use the Aperture mobile templates.

To add mobile pages to the Assets tab:

1. On the **Assets** tab, click the **Pages** category header and then click 🗀 **Browse**.

   The Asset Browser opens displaying all available pre-designed pages. We'll slim this down using a search.

2. In the **Asset Browser**, in the Search box, type 'Aperture'.

All pages with the **Aperture** tag are displayed.

3. In the Aperture - Mobile gallery, click the first two pages. The page assets are imported into the **Assets** tab.

The green shows that the asset has been added to the tab.

4. Click **Close**.

Now we'll add these pages to our site.

Asset tags are displayed by hovering the mouse over the asset thumbnail.

To add a new asset page (and its Master page):

1. On the **Assets** tab, on the **Pages** category, ensure the **Drag Master** option is selected.

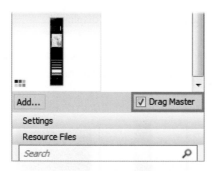

This ensures a new Master page is added to the site when a new asset page is added.

2. On the **Site** tab, double-click the **Terms & Conditions** page entry to open it in the workspace.

3. Drag the **Home** tagged mobile asset page from the **Assets** tab onto the workspace, and drop it (by releasing the mouse button) to the right of the current page when a large arrow appears.

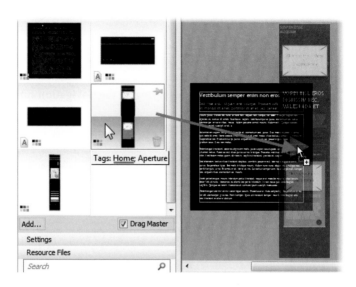

The page is displayed in the workspace added after the current page in the Site tab, listed as 'Page 10'.

Next, we'll rename this page to reflect the fact it is a mobile version of the Home page. We'll also exclude it from site navigation bars so it will not be automatically added to navigation bars.

To rename a page:

1. On the **Site** tab, right-click **Page 10** and select **Page Properties**.

2. In the **Page Properties** dialog, in the **Navigation** category:

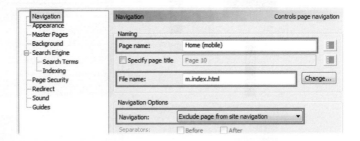

- In the **Page name** input box, type 'Home (mobile)'. This allows you to identify your mobile pages.

- In the **File name** input box, change the default file name to 'm.index.html' (see note below). This allows search engines to identify your mobile pages.

- From the **Navigation** drop-down list, select **Exclude page from site navigation**.

- Click **OK**.

The page updates in the Site tab.

It is a standard internet convention to use the file name **index.html** for a website's main (usually Home) page. By using **m.index.html** for this mobile page, it identifies it as being the main page for your mobile website.

Let's add another mobile template page...

To add a new asset page (without a Master page):

1. On the **Assets** tab, on the **Pages** category, uncheck the **Drag Master** option.

   A new Master page will no longer be added when a new asset page is added.

2. Drag the **Contact Us** tagged mobile asset page from the **Assets** tab onto the workspace, and drop it (by releasing the mouse button) to the right of the current page when a large arrow appears.

   The page is displayed in the workspace and listed as Page 11 in the Site tab. This page does not have a Master page assigned to it.

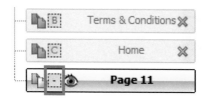

We'll assign the same Master page to it as we have on the Home (mobile) page when we rename it.

To assign a Master page to a page:

1. On the **Site** tab, right-click **Page 11** and select **Page Properties**.

2. In the **Page Properties** dialog, in the **Navigation** category:

   - In the **Page name** input box, type 'Contact Us (mobile)'.

   - In the **File name** input box, change the default file name to 'm.contactus.html'.

   - From the **Navigation** drop-down list, select **Exclude page from site navigation**.

3. In the **Master Pages** category, select **Master C**.

This is the Master page which is also attached to the mobile Home page.

4. Click **OK**.

The Contact Us page adopts all the elements of Master C.

Next, we'll walk through modifying the navigation bar on your Master page to prevent confusing website visitors.

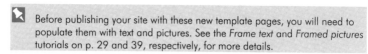

Before publishing your site with these new template pages, you will need to populate them with text and pictures. See the *Frame text* and *Framed pictures* tutorials on p. 29 and 39, respectively, for more details.

Save now! Click **File > Save As**.

Modifying navigation bars

You'll notice the navigation bar on your mobile pages display a green exclamation mark. This is because the navigation bar lists all site pages rather than just the appropriate mobile pages. We can modify the navigation bar on the Master page so it only displays the mobile pages.

To modify a navigation bar:

1. Select the navigation bar and then, from the object toolbar, select  **Edit on Master Page**.

    Master C Master page will display in the workspace with the navigation bar selected.

2. On the context toolbar, click **Edit Navigation Bar**.

3. In the **Edit Navigation Bar** dialog, on the **Navigation Type** tab, select **Custom**.

The default site structure is displayed. We'll modify this to create a unique navigation bar for our mobile pages.

To customize a navigation bar:

1. In the **Edit Navigation Bar** dialog, on the **Navigation Type** tab, click **Delete All** and then click **OK** to remove all the page entries from the navigation bar.

2. With the **Empty** entry selected, click **Edit Link**.

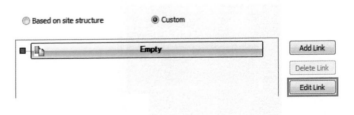

3. In the **Edit Hyperlink** dialog, on the **Custom Navigation Tree Item**, drag to select the 'Empty' **Menu name** and type 'Home'.

Custom Navigation Tree Item	Hyperlink	Actions

Navigation Settings

Menu name: Home

This keeps the page naming in the navigation bar consistent with the main website.

4. On the **Hyperlink Type** tab (**Hyperlink** tab):

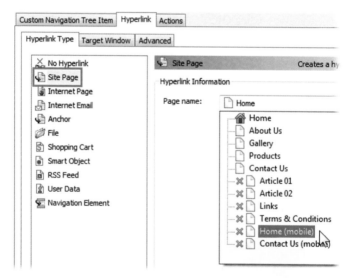

- Select the **Site Page** category.

- In the **Page name** drop-down list, select **Home (mobile)**.

- Click **OK**.

5. Back in the **Edit Navigation Bar** dialog, click **Add Link**.

6. In the **Edit Hyperlink** dialog, on the **Custom Navigation Tree Item**, in the **Menu name** input box, type 'Contact Us'.

7. On the **Hyperlink Type** tab (**Hyperlink** tab):

   • Select the **Site Page** category.

   • In the **Page name** drop-down list, select **Contact Us (mobile)**.

   • Click **OK**.

     Back in the **Edit Navigation Bar** dialog, the navigation structure has been updated.

8. Click **OK**.

The navigation bar updates to display the custom navigation bar.

 If you add any additional mobile pages, you will need to manually update the navigation bar on the Master page (as described above).

Let's check our progress by previewing the website as if it were displayed on a mobile phone.

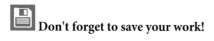 **Don't forget to save your work!**

To preview your site in WebPlus:

1.    On the **Standard** toolbar, click the arrow to expand the **Preview site** drop-down list.

2.   Click the **Preview in Window (Internet Explorer)** option.

   WebPlus displays the site preview in a built-in Microsoft Internet Explorer window.

3.   Click the Page Locator at the bottom left of the workspace, and select **Home (mobile)**.

4. On the context toolbar, from the drop-down list, select **Custom**.

5. In the dialog, set the **Width** to **340 pix** and click **OK**.

6. When you have finished previewing your site, click  **Close Preview**.

We've set up the navigation *between* the mobile pages but currently there is no way for visitors to access them. We can set up redirects so the correct pages display depending on the type of device a visitor is using.

Setting up page redirects

Setting up page redirects is a quick and easy process in WebPlus. First, we'll show you how to redirect visitors from the main Home page to the mobile version, if they access the website from a portable device.

To redirect to a mobile page:

1. On the **Site** tab, right-click **Home** and select **Page Properties**.

2. In the **Page Properties** dialog, in the **Redirect** category, click **Link** next to the **Redirect to** box.

3. In the **Edit Page Redirect** dialog:

- Select the **Site Page** category.

- From the **Page name** drop-down list, select **Home (mobile)**.

- Click **OK**.

4. Select **Redirect only on condition** option and then select **If recognised mobile device**.

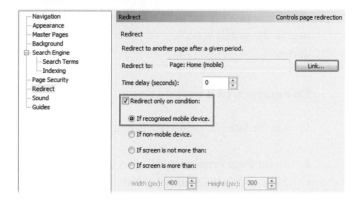

5. Click **OK**.

Now, when a visitor access the main Home page (index.html) from a mobile device they will be immediately redirected to the mobile version (m.index.html).

However, we also need to consider the reverse scenario. We should ideally set up a redirect to the main Home page if a visitor accidently accesses the mobile version from their desktop or laptop computer.

Don't forget to save your work!

To redirect to a non-mobile page:

1. On the **Site** tab, right-click **Home (mobile)** and select **Page Properties**.

2. In the **Page Properties** dialog, in the **Redirect** category, click **Link** next to the **Redirect to** box.

3. In the **Edit Page Redirect** dialog:

   - Select the **Site Page** category.

   - From the **Page name** drop-down list, select **Home**.

   - Click **OK**.

4. Select **Redirect only on condition** option and then select **If non-mobile device**.

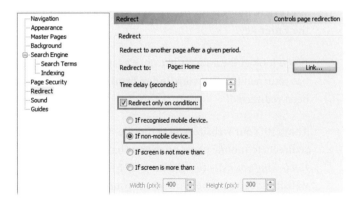

5. Click **OK**.

Now, when a visitor accidently accesses the mobile Home page (m.index.html) from a desktop or laptop computer they will be immediately redirected to the main version (index.html).

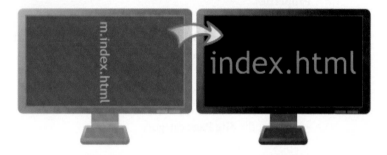

We'll leave you to follow the above procedures to set up redirects between Contact Us and Contact Us (mobile).

You can test the above redirect by previewing your site in a browser. See *To preview your site in a browser* on p. 8 for details.

In the address bar at the top of the browser, modify the address from '../Preview/index.html' to '../Preview/m.index.html' and then press the **Enter** key.

If you look at the address bar once again, you will notice the address has returned to **../Preview/index.html** meaning you have already been redirected!

That's it! Your website is now mobile-ready. You can test the redirects to mobile pages once your have published your site (see the *Publishing your site* tutorial on p. 171 for details). Simply type your website address in the browser on your mobile device and you'll see the mobile version of you Home page display!

Instead of using pre-designed mobile template pages, you can create your own mobile pages based on previously created pages. We've included an extra section below which walks you through the procedure.

 Don't forget to save your work!

Creating mobile pages from previously created site pages

You can create mobile pages for your site from previously created site pages. First you'll need to clone the site page and then modify it for displaying on mobile devices. We'll show you how...

To clone a page:

1. On the **Site** tab, right-click **Home** and select **Clone Page**.

    The cloned page is added to the site and placed under the original page in the **Site** tab.

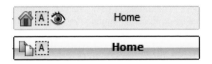

2. On the **Site** tab, right-click the cloned **Home** and select **Page Properties**.

3. In the **Page Properties** dialog, in the **Navigation** category:

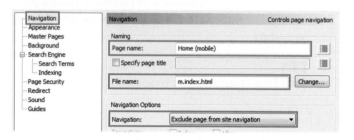

- In the **Page name** input box, type 'Home (mobile)'.

  This allows you to identify your mobile pages.

- In the **File name** input box, change the default file name to 'm.index.html' (see note below).

  This allows search engines to identify your mobile pages.

- From the **Navigation** drop-down list, select **Exclude page from site navigation**.

 It is a standard internet convention to use the file name **index.html** for a website's main (usually Home) page. By using **m.index.html** for this mobile page, it identifies it as being the main page for your mobile website.

4. In the **Appearance** category, set the **Width** to **320 pix**.

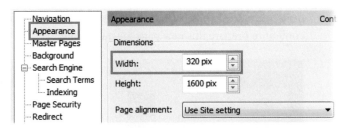

5. Click **OK**.

You can repeat the above procedure to create more if you wish.

As an alternative, you may wish to create new mobile pages from scratch. To do so, on the **Site** tab, click the down arrow next to 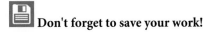 **Add new page or link** and select **New Blank Page** and then follow steps 3 and 4 above.

Don't forget to save your work!

If you navigate to your new **Home (mobile)** page it is likely you will see the content is no longer neatly positioned on the page. You may need to lengthen your page, resize your page objects, or remove content to prepare this new page for publishing.

If the current Master page design doesn't work for your mobile pages, you may wish to create a new Master page to attach to your mobile pages (or clone the Master page as above) or use a pre-designed mobile template Master page (available from the **Assets Browser**).

Publishing your site

 25 min

Once you have made your site, the next step is to publish it to the internet. We'll take you through the steps in this tutorial.

By the end of this tutorial you will be able to:

- Prepare your website for publication.

- Set up your FTP account.

- Publish and maintain your website.

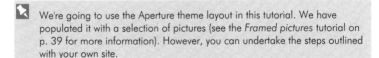

We're going to use the Aperture theme layout in this tutorial. We have populated it with a selection of pictures (see the *Framed pictures* tutorial on p. 39 for more information). However, you can undertake the steps outlined with your own site.

Let's begin...

- Open the **Aperture** template as described on p. 4.

 If you have already completed the previous tutorial, you can use your saved project for this tutorial.

Preparing your website for publication

There are several checks you may wish to make before your website is published on the internet.

To prepare your website for web publication:

1. Preview the site in WebPlus and in various web browsers. See *Previewing your website* on p. 6 for details.

2. Check your page names, file names, and picture export settings in the **Properties** > **Site Properties** and **Tools** > **Image Export Manager** dialogs. (For details, search *Setting image export options* in WebPlus Help.)

3. Use **Site Checker** (**Tools** > **Site Manager**) to check your site for problems such as non-websafe fonts, invalid anchors and hyperlinks, and so on. (For details, search *Using site checker* in WebPlus Help.)

Uppercase letters, spaces and symbols in file names can cause problems when visitors access your published website. WebPlus can overcome these issues by converting file names when your site is uploaded to the web.

To convert file names:

1. On the **Properties** menu, click **Site Properties**.

2. In the **Site Properties** dialog:

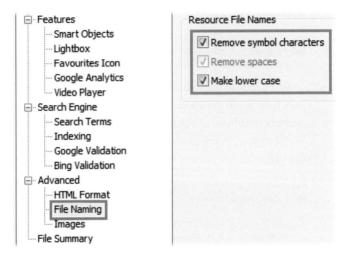

- Click **Advanced>File Naming**.

- Select the **Remove symbol character** or **Remove spaces** option.

- Select **Make lower case** to allow WebPlus to convert file names to lower case for you.

- Click **OK**.

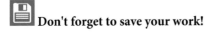 **Don't forget to save your work!**

When you are satisfied all issues with your website have been resolved, you can set up your FTP account and publish to the world wide web.

Setting up your FTP account

 You will only have to set up your FTP account the first time you publish your site to the web.

Now it's time to publish our site to a live location. Even though you may have saved your website as a WebPlus project, it's not truly a 'website' until you've converted it to files that can be viewed in a Web browser. WebPlus does this automatically when you publish the site.

 Useful terms to know:

• **FTP** - File Transfer Protocol—this is the standard way of uploading your website's files from your computer to your web host.

• **URL** - Universal Resource Locator—this is the 'address' where your site resides on the web.

• **Web Host** - this is a company which provides web space for you to store the files necessary to display your website pages on the internet.

 The next steps assume that you have dedicated space on a web server. If you are unsure how to access this, contact your Web host.

To set up your FTP account:

1. On the **Standard** toolbar, click the arrow to expand the **Publish site** drop-down list.

2. Click **Publish to Web**.

3. In the **Publish To Web: Get Hosting** dialog, click **Add Details**.

4. In the **Site Base URL** dialog, type in the URL for your website in the text box, e.g. http://www.golfingestate.com.

    The **Account Details** dialog will open.

5. When publishing to the Web you'll need to provide the following information, which you can obtain from your Web host. (When you receive this information, usually displayed on-screen or sent by email on purchase of your web space, it is worth printing out for your own records and for later reference.)

Details	
Account name:	Golfing Estate
FTP address:	ftp.golfingestate.com
Port number:	21 (Default FTP port 21, unless in implied mode)
Folder:	(May be case-sensitive)
Username:	golfingestate
Password:	●●●●●●●●●●●● ☑ Save password
Passive mode:	☑ (Uncheck this if you have problems connecting)
Web site URL:	http://www.golfingestate (optional)

- **Account name:** A descriptive name for this connection. This can be any name of your choice. You'll use it to identify this account in WebPlus (you may have more than one).

- **FTP address:** The URL that locates the server that will store your files—it will look similar to a Web address but often starts 'ftp://'. The FTP address is supplied by your Web host.

- **Port number:** Leave the **Port number** set at 21, unless directed by your Web host.

- **Folder:** Allows you to upload sites to sub-folders of your main website's address. You can leave this blank unless you are directed otherwise by your Web host, or you want to publish to a specific subfolder of your root directory. (This may also be needed to correctly route your upload specifically to your own Web space.)

- **Username:** Specified by your Web host—often case-sensitive.

- **Password:** Specified by your Web host—often case-sensitive.

- **Passive Mode:** Leave checked (by default) unless you experience upload problems.

- **Website URL:** The web address of your site—often starts 'http://' or 'https://'.

- Click **OK**.

 For more information about setting up your account details, search *Publishing to the web* in WebPlus Help.

Before you proceed further, it's a good idea to test your account settings to ensure there are no issues with connecting to the internet.

To test your account details and connection:

- In the **Upload to server** dialog, click **Test**.

  WebPlus will attempt to connect to your hosting account.

  You will be informed if the connection has been successful:

  - If unsuccessful, select your FTP Account from the drop-down list and click **Edit** to review your settings.

  - If successful, click **Update Account**—your new FTP account and settings are displayed in the **Publish to Web** dialog. (Your FTP account details are saved for future use.)

Once you've set up your FTP account and can connect your computer to the host, publishing to the Web is simply a matter of transferring files.

Publishing to the web

With your FTP account set up and project ready-to-go, let's get onto the exciting task of getting your site onto the web!

 If you're currently in the main workspace, click **File>Publish Site>Publish to Web** to access the **Publish to Web** dialog.

To publish your site to the web:

1. In the **Publish to Web** dialog, your current FTP account details should be displayed. If not, select an FTP account from the drop-down list.

2. In the **Page Range** tree, select which page(s) to publish. To publish the entire site, select the **Publish All Pages** option.

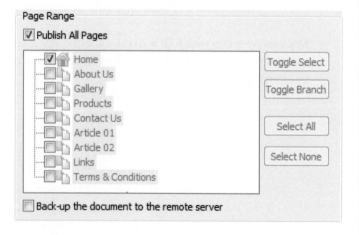

3. Click **OK**.

WebPlus will convert your design into HTML pages with associated graphics and other files, then begin to upload your site to the internet, showing individual file progress and overall progress.

4. When WebPlus has exported the selected pages, close the **Uploading files** dialog—the **Web Site Publishing** dialog opens.

5. To view your site online, choose your browser from the drop-down list and click **View this URL**.

Your browser will launch showing the specified URL.

Now that your website is live on the web. Let's take a quick look at how you update and maintain it.

 Don't forget to save your work!

Maintaining your website

The great thing about websites is the ability to update them frequently at no extra cost—in fact, visitors will expect your website to be up-to-date with all the latest information. With WebPlus, it's quick to update a modified website which has been previously published.

To update a previously published website:

1. With your WebPlus project still open in your workspace, use the Page Locator at the bottom left of the workspace to select the **Home** page.

2. Make any necessary changes to the page.

   We updated a couple of the text frames.

See the *Frame text* tutorial on p. 29 for more details.

Don't forget to save your work!

3. From the **File** menu, click **Publish Site** and then select **Publish to Web**.

4. In the **Publish To Web** dialog:

   - Select an FTP account from the drop-down list.

   - In the **Page Range** section, ensure only the **Home** page is selected.

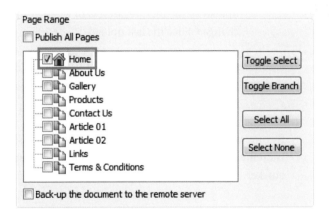

   - Click **OK**.

5. In the Uploading Files dialog, select **Incremental Update** or **Full Upload**.

- **Incremental Update:** If you choose this option, WebPlus will export your site and compare the exported files to those already on the server. It will only upload files that are new or have changed since the last upload. This option can also check for missing files. Incremental updates are great when you want to quickly replace minor elements of your site!

- **Full Upload:** If you choose this option, WebPlus will upload all the files, regardless of whether they have changed since the last upload.

  In both cases you can instruct WebPlus to delete uploaded files that are no longer required by selecting this option in the dialog.

By only uploading pages which have changed (and selecting **Incremental Update**) you will notice that the web upload is much quicker.

You can view your updated page in a browser.

 You can maintain your published website further by using the **Maintain Website** dialog (accessible from **File>Publish Site**). For more information, search *Maintaining your website* in WebPlus Help.

That's it! You've published your site to the web for all to see! As you can see, WebPlus makes it very easy to publish your site and upload new content.

If you're having problems we suggest you check your provider's website to find the information you need, or contact their customer support team.

Note: Serif cannot supply you with this information unless you have a Serif web hosting account.

Search Engine Optimization (SEO)

 30 min

This tutorial will help you develop good techniques which should help improve your website's visibility on search engines.

By the end of this tutorial you will be able to:

- Use page names, titles, and file names to improve searches.

- Use keywords and descriptions effectively.

- Understand how good website content can improve results.

- Generate search engine files.

- Submit your site to search engines.

What is Search Engine Optimization?

A search engine is an internet-based tool which aids a user in finding specific information. Search Engine Optimization (or SEO) is a process of optimizing your website to help increase its popularity and ranking across search results, without the need to purchase advertising slots. A website that appears towards the top of a list of results will encourage users to click the link. Spending time optimizing your website is definitely worth considering if you want to drive traffic to it.

SEO is not necessary for every website and there are other internet marketing strategies that can be as effective in generating traffic to your site. Your website doesn't have to appear in search engine rankings for people to access it once a site is live; if your visitors already know your website's web address (URL) they can access it directly using the address bar at the top of their internet browser. SEO is particularly helpful in acquiring new website visitors that are interest-matched to your products, services, the information on your site, and sometimes your location.

Our main aim in this tutorial is to make your website 'search engine friendly', using proven techniques as recommended by search engine operators.

Let's begin...

* Open the **Aperture** template as described on p. 4.

If you have already completed the previous tutorial, you can use your saved project for this tutorial.

Now let's see if we can make your site search engine friendly.

Making your site search engine friendly

To help get you noticed, there are recommended strategies that you can use to make your website search engine friendly.

We cannot tell you how to get your site ranked high in search engine results. Search engine companies carefully guard their algorithms on creating results to prevent people 'cheating' their way up the listings.

Linking

Hyperlinks to external web pages, other pages on your site, and anchors on long pages are analyzed by search engine technologies and will add weight to your content's credibility.

If you work frequently with specific businesses and clients, or have family and friends with websites, why not link to their websites and ask them to link to yours—network via the net!

See the *Creating hyperlinks and anchors* tutorial on p. 53 for more information on adding hyperlinks and anchors to your own website.

HTML tags

Text frames offer you the ability to design with HTML-compliant styles. This means that you can format text using heading styles from H1 to H6. H*n* styles are given priority over ordinary body text styles (the default) in internet search engines, with the H1 tag being given highest priority.

To apply an HTML meta tag to a style:

1. On the **Text Styles** tab, move the mouse pointer over the **Heading 1** style and click the down-arrow.

2. Click **Modify Heading 1**.

3. In the **Text Style** dialog:

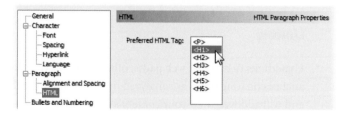

- Click the **Paragraph** category and select the **HTML** sub-category.

- Select the appropriate HTML tag (in this case **H1** is already selected).

- Click **OK.**

The **H1** tag will be applied whenever the **Heading 1** style is used within a text frame.

 The **Text Styles** tab contains preset Heading styles which translate to HTML tags **H1** to **H6**. You can format the text style to suit your site design while keeping those important tags.

See the *Frame text* tutorial on p. 37 for more information on assigning text styles.

ALT and TITLE tags

It's possible to add some HTML text tags (**ALT** and **TITLE** tags) to your pictures and other objects that will be published as images. Using pertinent keywords for these text strings adds further weight to your site's content.

See the *Framed pictures* tutorial on p. 39 for more information on assigning ALT and TITLE tags.

Page names, titles and file names

In WebPlus, there are three ways of identifying each page: **name**, **title**, and **file name**. Each of these works differently to help search engines list your website pages:

- **Name**: is not directly used by search engines, but becomes the default page title, if a title is not provided.

- **Title**: is stored both in the published HTML code (for use by search engines) and in the visible title bar of viewers' Web browsers.

- **File name**: is used by search engines to distinguish pages and is usually displayed at the end of the website URL.

When you add a new page to your site, you will be given the option to add a custom name, title and file name. Alternatively, you can update the page name, title, and file name of existing pages by right-clicking the page in the **Site** tab and selecting **Page Properties**.

Strong page names, titles, and file names work particularly well alongside site and page keywords and descriptions. Together they provide a wealth of information to help search engines identify and categorize your website—as well as strengthening your site's credentials.

Keywords and site description

When choosing **keywords**, think about your site and its content. Do a little research to help you find out what keywords people would search with to find your site, as well as thinking about what you offer in particular. Also note variations of UK and US English words.

It's important that your keywords appear in the site content as well, otherwise this can be seen as keyword stuffing—a less reputable SEO technique that can actually result in your site being ranked lower than it otherwise would be. Having carefully chosen a set of keywords, let's integrate them into your site.

To set keywords for a site:

1.   From the **Properties** menu, select **Site Properties**.

2.   In the **Site Properties** dialog:

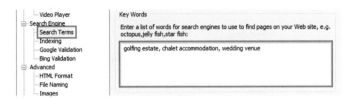

- Click the **Search Engine>Search Terms** category.

- Type your keywords in the **Key Words** text box. Separate your keywords and keyword phrases with commas.

- Click **OK**.

The site-wide keywords you enter will be included on each page of your site.

> Here are some simple rules to consider when creating keywords:
>
> • Keep them focused.
>
> • Ensure they represent your site and page content accurately.
>
> • All your site keywords **must** appear somewhere in your site text content.

If you have a multi-page site and certain pages offer unique content, you can supplement the keyword and description information on a page-by-page basis. Remember, any keywords you add per page must appear somewhere in your page's text content.

To set keywords for a page:

1. On the **Site** tab, right-click the 'Home' page and click **Page Properties**.

2. In the **Page Properties** dialog:

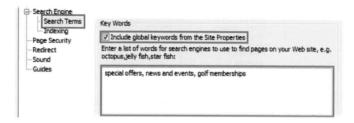

- Click the **Search Engine>Search Terms** category.

- To include keywords and phrases from your Site Properties, ensure **Include global keywords from the Site Properties** is selected.

- Type your choice of keywords in the **Key Words** text box. Separate your keywords and keyword phrases with commas.

- Click **OK**.

Having page-specific keywords and descriptions that better match the body text on each page will help improve your site's chances of a higher search engine ranking.

Site and page description

The site and page descriptions are used by search engines to help determine a rank for your site among search results—it also appears below the hyperlinks in searches, giving users an idea of what displays on the site and page. Aim to have a clear, concise description.

Here are some simple rules to consider when creating descriptions:

- Keep it clear, informative, and concise, and ensure it represents your site and page content accurately.

- It should contain your chosen keywords and keyword phrases, but should not excessively repeat them.

- Use correct spelling, punctuation, and sentence structure, while also avoiding acronyms.

- Use "and" not "&", unless the sentence normally appears with "&" on your site.

You can enter your site and page descriptions in the **Search Terms** category in the **Site Properties** and **Page Properties** dialogs.

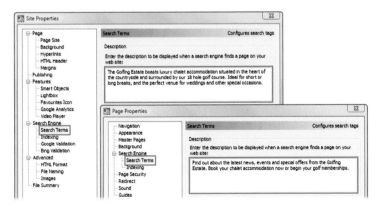

You may wish to write your site/page description first, and then pick out keywords within the description.

To preview your site in a browser:

1. Preview the site in a browser. See *To preview your site in a browser* on p. 8 for details.

2. In your browser, choose to view '**Source**' (usually available from the browser's **View** menu or from a right-click menu).

```
8    <meta name="keywords" content="special offers, news and events,
     golf memberships, golfing estate, chalet accommodation, wedding
     venue">
9    <meta name="description" content="Find out about the latest
     news, events and special offers from the Golfing Estate. Book your
     chalet accommodation now or begin your golf memberships.">
```

As you can see from our coloured HTML snippet, the keywords and description are stored in a meta tag—a named piece of information within the HTML code.

 Keywords and other search engine related tweaks can also be accessed via the **Site Manager**. For more information about either the Site Manager or assigning keywords to your site, search *Using Site Manager* in WebPlus Help.

Many search engines, including Google™, do not use meta tag keywords in their search engine technology, so you'll need to go beyond the WebPlus Site and Page Properties dialogs. This can include writing focused text content.

Text content

The **text content** of each page is crucial. Writing engaging content can have a big impact on improving search results! Make sure your chosen site keywords are well represented throughout your site and page keywords appear within the text on your page. Including keywords in the first paragraph of a page is of particular importance.

In addition to writing finer detail in your content, you should also include broader descriptions and terms frequently. You may also like to ensure important words in your text appear in **bold** or *italic* formatting, and give them prominence in a page's first text paragraph. These attributes may lead to those words being given more prominence in search rankings.

It's not difficult to write content with the keywords in mind. Using your keywords in your main text can also make up for any key terms which are published as part of a graphic—search engines can't read text that has been converted to a picture.

 You may wish to write your site/page text content first, and then pick out important sections to create your site/page descriptions and keywords.

Some search engine companies use automated systems (often called **spiders**) to find and help rank sites. These electronic arachnids follow links to your site from known resources (or find your site in the search engine's own directory) and analyze your site's keywords as well as other content. Let's explore this further…

Search engine file generation

Web crawlers discover pages from links within your website. Sitemap.xml supplements this data and allows crawlers to pick up all of the URLs. Essentially, sitemap.xml is a list of all of the pages that you really want indexing and provides extra information about each URL, such as how often the page changes, when it was last updated, how important it is compared to the other site pages, etc.

All of this information can really improve your site rankings— WebPlus takes care of writing the file for you.

To create a sitemap.xml file:

1. On the **Properties** menu, click **Site Properties**.

2. In the **Site Properties** dialog, click the **Search Engine>Indexing** category, then:

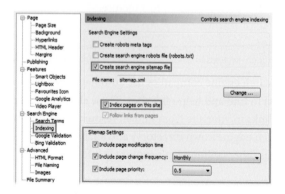

- Select the **Create search engine sitemap file** option.

  We recommended you do not change the file name.

- Select **Index pages on this site** and choose which **Sitemap Settings** you wish to apply.

  If you want to display page priority, remember 0.0 is the lowest and 1.0 is the highest setting. The page priority set in this dialog will be set as a default to all site pages.

- Click **OK**.

3. If the **Site Base URL** dialog appears, click **Cancel** for now.

Individual pages on the site can be given different settings to the rest of the site, or be entirely excluded from the sitemap file.

To modify a sitemap.xml file for individual pages:

1. On the **Site** tab, right-click the 'Home' page and click **Page Properties**.

2. In the **Page Properties** dialog:

- Click the **Search Engine>Indexing** category.

- Select the **Override site search engine settings** option.

- Update the settings as appropriate and then click **OK**.

Whereas sitemap.xml tells the Web crawler to index the page and follow its links, **robots.txt** does the opposite. Essentially, it provides a list of pages that should not be indexed. This can be useful if you do not want to include one or more links that go to external sites. Robots.txt generally works in conjunction with the robots meta tags for more precise settings. For more information, search *Search Engine Optimization* in WebPlus Help.

To create a robots.txt file:

1. On the **Properties** menu, click **Site Properties**.

2. Click the **Search Engine>Indexing** category:

   - Select the **Create search engine robots file (robots.txt)** option.

   - Click **OK**.

3. If the **Site Base URL** dialog appears, click **Cancel** for now.

For the overall site properties, it is best to leave the **Index pages on this site** option selected. If you have a page that you do not want to index, you can do this from the **Site Manager** dialog.

A good page to remove from indexing would be a Search Results page.

To exclude a page from index:

1. From the Tools menu, select **Site Manager>Page Properties**.

2. In the **Site Manager** dialog, click the **Page Properties>Indexing** category, then:

   - Ensure **Override Site** is checked for the page that you do not want to index.

   - Uncheck **Index Page**.

3. Click **Close**.

In addition to all the preparation you've made directly to your website, some search engine companies accept submissions of sites for inclusion in their search results, sometimes at a price. This may be a handy strategy for improving traffic to your website if needed.

Search engine submissions

You can submit your website (generally for free) to popular search engines (such as Google and Bing) to help get your website listed. The engines will then use "crawlers" to index your site. Detailed information about submitting your site to search engines can be found on the internet.

In addition, you should try to get your site listed in the free online directory called the **Open Directory Project**, www.dmoz.org.

We've only scratched the surface here on optimizing your website for inclusion in search engine listings—the internet has many other tips and tricks to help you along. Furthermore, search engine technology is constantly evolving and becoming ever more complex. The main thing to remember is that keeping your website up to date with engaging content is really the best way of optimizing your website. Best of luck!

The tips throughout this tutorial have focused on honest methods of improving rankings (known as 'White Hat SEO') rather than devious methods (known as 'Black Hat SEO') which can actually harm search engine rankings. Try searching on "Black Hat vs White Hat SEO" using your favourite search engine for more information and tips.

Creative
Showcase

2

Pro Templates

WebPlus provides a selection of **Pro Templates** that are populated
with pictures and text placeholders.

To open Pro Templates:

1. On the **File** menu, click **Startup Assistant**.

2. On the left, click **Templates**.

3. On the **Templates** list, select **WebPlus X7 Pro Templates**, and
    click to select one of the templates.

4. Click **OK**.

You'll find the **Alleberry Bed & Breakfast**, **Beach House Lifestyle**
and **Villereccio Pizzeria** templates showcased on the following
pages.

 You can get more **Pro Templates** from Serif's template store. Visit
http://www.serif.com/templates/webplus

Alleberry Bed & Breakfast

Beach House Lifestyle

Villereccio Pizzeria

Theme Layouts

WebPlus provides a selection of **Theme Layout** templates with picture and text placeholders that you can use as starting points for your own sites.

To open a theme layout site:

1. On the **File** menu, click **Startup Assistant**.

2. On the left, click **Templates**.

3. On the **Templates** list, select **Theme Layouts**, and click to select a thumbnail.

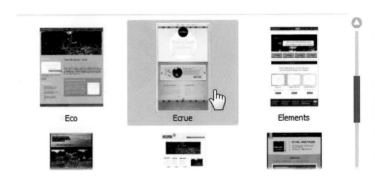

4. Click **OK**.

You'll find the **Ecrue**, **Kitsch**, **Tessellate**, **Prospectus – Mobile**, and **Warehouse – Mobile** theme layouts showcased on the following pages. We have added a picture to the placeholder picture frames for clarity.

Ecrue

Kitsch

Tessellate

Prospectus – Mobile

Warehouse – Mobile

Assets and object styles

WebPlus comes installed with assets which you can quickly add to your site pages to build up content and pre-designed object styles which can be applied to objects.

Assets

WebPlus assets, available from the **Assets Browser** and **Assets** tab, range from individual objects to full page designs. Assets are organized into the following categories: **Graphics**, **Pictures**, **Page Content**, **Pages**, **Settings** and **Resource Files**.

For more information on using assets, see *New site from template*, on p. 3.

You'll find the **Graphics** and **Page Content** assets showcased on p. 214 and p. 215.

Object styles

The **Styles** tab provides you with pre-designed object styles which you can apply to any object on your page.

For more information on using object styles, see *Object styles* on p. 81.

We'll showcase the **Preset - Defaults** category on p. 216.

Graphics – Heirloom

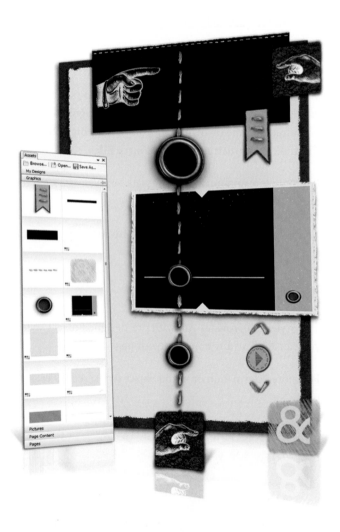

Page Content – Elements

Preset - Defaults

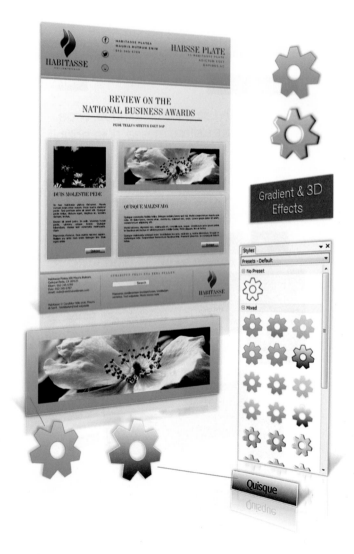